Reading Group Choices

Selections for Lively Book Discussions

Paz & Associates

2000

© 2000 Paz & Associates
All Rights Reserved.
Published in the United States by Paz & Associates.

For further information, contact:
Donna Paz, Publisher
Mark Kaufman, Editor
Reading Group Choices
Paz & Associates
2106 Twentieth Avenue South
Nashville, TN 37212-4312

800/260-8605 — phone
615/298-9864 — fax
mkaufman@pazbookbiz.com — email

Visit our websites at:
www.readinggroupchoices.com
www.pazbookbiz.com

ISBN 0-9644876-5-9

Cover design: Mary Caprio

Printed by:
Rich Printing Company, Inc.
7131 Centennial Bl.
Nashville, TN 37209
615/350-7300

A portion of the proceeds from this publication will be used to support literacy efforts throughout the United States.

This publication is dedicated to the authors, agents, publishers, book distributors, and booksellers who bring us books that enrich our lives.

ACKNOWLEDGMENTS

This sixth edition of *Reading Group Choices* offers an exciting and thought-provoking mix of titles and topics, exploring issues like a sense of place, the impact of war, cultural identity, parenting, contempory history and more – in addition to an eclectic and exciting collection of fiction. What better proof that books can change lives!

We wish to thank our publishing colleagues who continue to support this publication and bring readers quality books for group discussion:

Algonquin Books of Chapel Hill	Allen A. Knoll
Aralon Press	Avon Books
Broadway Books (Random House)	Curbstone Press
Bantam Doubleday Dell	Harcourt Brace
Louisiana State Univesity Press	MacMurray and Beck
Milkweed Editions	Owl Books (Henry Holt)
Pelican Publishing	Picador (St. Martin's Press)
Plough Publishing	Putnam Publishing Group
Scribner (Simon & Schuster)	Spinsters Ink
Starnes Publishing	University of Missouri Press
University Press of Kentucky	VanderWyk & Burnham
Vintage Books (Random House)	W. H. Freeman
Williams Hill Publishing	

A special thanks to our Advisory Board of readers, reading discussion group leaders, librarians, and booksellers who shared their expertise and love of books to screen recommendations:

Jean Bolinger, *Book Nook*, Warren, Ohio
Kathleen Cotter, *The Queens Borough Public Library*, Jamaica, NY
Lynn Lockhart, *Black Bond Books*, Surrey, B.C.
Barbara Theroux, *Fact & Fiction*, Missoula, MT

For their assistance in creating discussion topics for several of the books in this edition, we wish to thank Lauren Baratz-Logsted, Megan DuBois, Barbara Richards Haugen, and Amy Lyles Wilson.

In appreciation of their ongoing alliance with Paz & Associates and their efforts in producing *Reading Group Choices*, we thank Mary Caprio for her cover design, and Rich Printing Company, quality book printers since 1892.

INTRODUCTION

If Chicken Little were still around, and had updated his message to "The world is shrinking, the world is shrinking!", would we be any more inclined to believe him? Avid readers and lovers of good "discussible" books know that the world is at your fingertips, not only with the click of a mouse, but the turn of a page as well.

Consider the possibilities in this year's edition. In *Are You Somebody?*, you can learn how one woman, Nuala O'Faolain, has helped shape social, cultural and governmental affairs in Ireland through her newspaper columns. Or, in *The Sky Unwashed*, how the residents of a small village near Chernobyl dealt with one of the worst environmental disasters of our time. Other titles afford you a glimpse of India, China, Guatemala, and a host of third-world countries through the eyes of Peace Corps writers in *Living on the Edge*.

If your horizons are already too expanded, you can read a book like *Mr. Phillips* to ponder what it means to have a sense of place or what life might be like in a small town like *Goodnight, Nebraska*. Other popular themes in this year's selection include heroic struggles, mother-daughter relationships, the effects of war, and the very meaning of life and death.

As you browse these pages, you'll find a wonderful assortment of fiction (some brand new, others, like *I Capture the Castle*, first published in 1948) and nonfiction, guaranteed to give you plenty to think about — and even more to discuss!

Keep in mind that a fair number of the discussion topics for titles featured this year have been excerpted from publishers' Reading Group Guides. To research additional topics, author comments, and reviews, we encourage you to visit the publishers' websites.

Whether your book group chooses to explore a distant culture, or look more deeply within our own, we trust that you'll enjoy the eclectic mix of titles presented herein.

Mark Kaufman and Donna Paz
Nashville, Tennessee
January, 2000

CONTENTS

ALMOST A WOMAN
by Esmeralda Santiago 12

AMY AND ISABELLE
by Elizabeth Strout 14

ARE YOU SOMEBODY?
by Nuala O'Faolain 16

BLU'S HANGING
by Lois-Ann Yamanaka 18

THE CAGE
by Audrey Schulman 20

CRACKING INDIA
by Bapsi Sidhwa 22

CREEKER: A WOMAN'S JOURNEY
by Linda Scott DeRosier 24

DREAMING UNDER A TON OF LIZARDS
by Marian Michener 26

EAST OF THE MOUNTAINS
by David Guterson 28

ENEMY OF THE AVERAGE
by Margaret Nicol 30

EVENING
by Susan Minot 32

FALLING LEAVES
by Adeline Yen Mah 34

FINAL STORM
by Lewis R. Walton 36

FINDING GRACE
by Mary Saracino 38

GARDENS IN THE DUNES
by Leslie Marmon Silko 40

THE GIANT'S HOUSE
by Elizabeth McCracken 42

CONTENTS (continued)

GOODNIGHT, NEBRASKA
    by Tom McNeal 44

THE HOURS
    by Michael Cunningham 46

HUMMINGBIRD HOUSE
    by Patricia Henley 48

I CAPTURE THE CASTLE
    by Dodie Smith 50

IN SESSION
    by Deborah A. Lott 52

INSANE SISTERS
    by Gregg Andrews 54

LEARNING FROM HANNAH
    by William H. Thomas, M.D. 56

LIVING ON THE EDGE
    by John Coyne 58

THE LOVE OF A GOOD WOMAN
    by Alice Munro 60

THE MANY LIVES AND SECRET SORROWS OF JOSEPHINE B.
    by Sandra Gulland 62

MR. PHILLIPS
    by John Lanchester 64

PEARS ON A WILLOW TREE
    by Leslie Pietryzk 66

PEEL MY LOVE LIKE AN ONION
    by Ana Castillo 68

A PLACE WITHOUT TWILIGHT
    by Peter Feibleman 70

CONTENTS (continued)

PRETZEL LOGIC
by Lisa Rogak 72

THE RED TENT
by Anita Diamant 74

ROSIE'S PLACE
by Andrea Cleghorn 76

SHE SAID YES
by Misty Bernall 78

THE SKY UNWASHED
by Irene Zabytko 80

SOMETHING'S NOT RIGHT
by Nancy Lelewer 82

STYGO
by Laura Hendrie 84

SUGAR LAND
by Joni Rodgers 86

SUMMER AT THE RESORT
by Henry Grady Starnes 88

SUNDAY YOU LEARN HOW TO BOX
by Bil Wright 90

TALES OF PASSION, TALES OF WOE
by Sandra Gulland 92

UNFORGOTTEN
by D. J. Meador 94

WHERE RIVER TURNS TO SKY
by Gregg Kleiner 96

ZABELLE
by Nancy Kricorian 98

CONTENTS (continued)

OTHER BOOKS OF INTEREST 100

RESOURCES 103

INDEX BY SUBJECT / INTEREST AREA 111

INDEX BY AUTHOR 113

INDEX BY GENRE 116

ABOUT READING GROUP CHOICES 118

ABOUT PAZ & ASSOCIATES 119

ALMOST A WOMAN

Author: Esmeralda Santiago
Publisher: Vintage Books
Website: www.vintagebooks.com/read
Available in:
Paperback, 336 pages. $12.00
(ISBN 0-375-70521-X)
Genre: Nonfiction/Memoir

Summary

At the age of thirteen Esmeralda Santiago must leave the familiarity, warmth, and vibrancy of Puerto Rico to live in a three-room apartment in Brooklyn shared by ten family members. Challenged by language barriers, cultural stereotypes, and her strict and fiercely protective mother, Esmeralda begins her triumphant struggle for identity and independence. By day she studies acting and interprets for the family at city welfare offices; by night she accompanies her mother and sister to Latin dance halls, but on such a short leash that she does not have her first date until age twenty. Undaunted, she makes up for lost time in a romantic apprenticeship that is at once hilarious and heartbreaking.

Recommended by: *The Miami Herald*

"A universal tale familiar to thousands of immigrants to this country, but made special by Santiago's simplicity and honesty."

Author Biography

Esmeralda Santiago is the eldest of eleven children. She spent her childhood in Puerto Rico, and moved to New York, at the age of thirteen, with her mother and siblings. Santiago is the author of two other memoirs, *When I Was Puerto Rican* and *Almost a Woman*. She lives in Westchester County, New York, with her husband and two children.

Topics to Consider

1. What effects did the family's many moves have on their outlook on life, their relationships to one another and to outsiders, and, in particular, on Esmeralda's developing character?

2. Is group identity, in a multicultural place like New York, seen to be primarily racial? National? Linguistic? Regional?

3. What does Mami mean by "Americanized," and why does the word have such negative connotations for her? Why is she so afraid of Esmeralda's becoming Americanized too?

4. What mixed messages about men, women, and love does Esmeralda pick up, as a child, from her parents? How does her mother's example affect her own early relationships with men and boys?

5. How, according to Santiago, do race relations and racial consciousness differ between Puerto Rico and New York? Have the racial attitudes and stereotypes encountered by Esmeralda in the 1960s changed over the ensuing decades? Are things better, worse, or much the same?

6. Mami has high expectations for her daughters. How do you feel about the discrepancy between her standards and her own past behavior?

7. How can you explain the fact that Esmeralda accepts the marriage proposal of Jurgen, a man she has known only a few hours, when by her own admission she is deeply distrustful of men in general?

8. How has the lack of a father during her formative years affected Esmeralda's life, her character, and her dealings with the rest of the world? How might her life have been different if her father had been present? How might she, as a person, have developed differently?

AMY AND ISABELLE

Author: Elizabeth Strout
Publisher: Vintage Books, 2000
Website: www.vintagebooks.com/read
Available in:
Paperback, 320 pages. $13.00
(ISBN 0-375-70519-8)
Genre: Fiction

Summary

In a small New England town, the arrival of Isabelle Goodrow and her infant daughter, Amy, stirs a bit of curiosity. Declaring she is a widow simply in search of a place to earn a living, Isabelle is accepted—if not embraced—by her neighbors. She works hard at her job at the mill, eventually rising to become secretary to the boss. She attends church regularly and cares for her daughter conscientiously. Now sixteen, Amy is shy and quiet, drawing the passing attention of others only because of her long, lush hair. But things are different with Mr. Robertson, her new math teacher. He seems to see something special in Amy, and their intimate after-school conversations fill a need Amy barely knew existed. Step by tentative step, Amy awakens to love and physical pleasure, and is swept across the line from childhood fantasy to adult passion. Their transgression, discovered by Isabelle's boss, marks a turning point in the lives of both Amy and Isabelle.

Recommended by: *San Francisco Chronicle*

"Stunning...Heartbreaking...This novelist is destined for great things."

Author Biography

Born in Maine, Elizabeth Strout now lives in New York City with her husband and daughter. She has been teaching literature and writing for ten years. Her fiction has appeared in *The New Yorker* and many other magazines. *Amy and Isabelle* is her first novel.

Topics to Consider

1. Isabelle comes to Shirley Falls in order to start a new life. How does her desire to re-create herself affect the way she is perceived by other people? How does it influence the way she raises Amy?

2. What role does Isabelle's "crush" on Avery Clark play in her life? How do her fantasies about being a loving wife to Avery compare to the way she treats Amy and runs their home? Which is the "real" Isabelle?

3. At first Mr. Robertson appears to be a motivational teacher. Are his teaching methods appropriate and effective? Is it possible for a high school teacher to be "cool" without overstepping the boundaries between student and teacher?

4. What impact does Isabelle's protectiveness have on Amy's character and her sense of self? How did Isabelle's own childhood shape her character, not only as a mother, but as a woman?

5. Why does Amy insist that she initiated the physical relationship? Is she only trying to protect Mr. Robertson, or does she have other reasons for taking the responsibility for what happened?

6. Mr. Robertson's seduction of Amy and his absolute disregard for the consequences of his act shock Isabelle. Do you think that Isabelle mishandles the situation or is Mr. Robertson incapable feeling shame or remorse?

7. How accurate is Amy's belief that her mother is angry because Amy found someone to love her? What would make Amy think that?

8. Amy and Isabelle's conflict is presented within the context of small town life. How do the events in the lives of the women at the mill enhance the book?

9. Do you think the novel would have unfolded differently if Amy and Isabelle had lived in a large city?

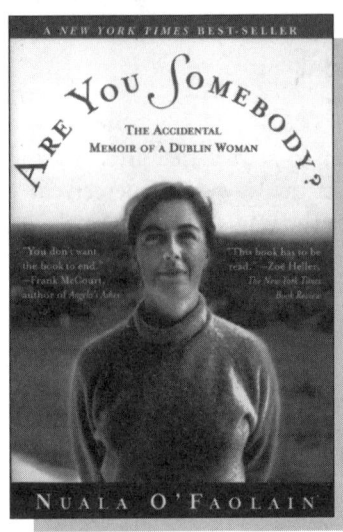

ARE YOU SOMEBODY?
The Accidental Memoir of a Dublin Woman

Author: Nuala O'Faolain
Publisher: Owl Books/Henry Holt
Website: www.henryholt.com
Available in:
Paperback, 215 pages. $11.95
(ISBN 0-8050-5664-5)
Genre: Nonfiction/Memoir

Summary

Irish Times columnist Nuala O'Faolain tells the story of being raised in Dublin by an alcoholic, overwhelmed mother and a feckless, absent father. Born into a penniless family, O'Faolain could have quietly composed her life within the confining boundaries of male-dominated Catholic Ireland. Instead, she plunges into her life, full of questions and wonder and fear. Against all odds she becomes both an agent and a beneficiary of change in Ireland, exposing the loneliness, passion, loss, love, pain, and self-discovery that have shaped her life.

Recommended by: Frank McCourt, author of *Angela's Ashes*

"You don't want the book to end: it glows with compassion and you want more, more because you know this is a fine wine of a life, richer as it ages."

Author Biography

Nuala O'Faolain has been a waitress, sales clerk, and maid; a university lecturer; a TV producer; and, most recently, a columnist with *The Irish Times*. She lives in Dublin.

Topics to Consider

1. Where does Nuala find values to live by? What role does her relationship with her parents play in Nuala's choice of values?

2. Although O'Faolain delights in romance, she has not married or settled into one long-term monogamous relationship. What has she lost and gained as a result?

3. How is Nuala able to escape the debilitating, overwhelming association with passion and love that undid her mother?

4. What kept Nuala in "the old culture", even after the women's movement had begun? What finally altered her perspective?

5. The author's age informs and colors her story. How might this memoir have differed had she written it either earlier or later in life?

6. What role do children play in the unfolding of Nuala's story? How are children betrayed by adults? What do children need from their parents? Why does Nuala believe that she would be a good parent at this stage in her life?

7. Discuss the ways in which Nuala's mother and father succeeded as parents.

8. O'Faolain has a complicated relationship with God — she both expresses her gratitude to God and denies God's existence in the same sentence. What is the source of her fierce ambivalence?

9. What meaning(s) does the title hold? The subtitle?

BLU'S HANGING

Author: Lois-Ann Yamanaka

Publisher:
Bard/Avon, 1998

Website: www.AvonBooks.com/Bard

Available in:
Paperback, 262 pages. $12.00
(ISBN 0-380-73139-8)

Genre: Fiction

Summary

On the Hawaiian island of Moloka'i, life goes on for the three young Ogata children after the death of their mother and the emotional withdrawal of their grief- and guilt-stricken "Poppy." The eldest at thirteen, "big sista" Ivah is now responsible for the safety and well being of her siblings: for little Maisie — electively mute since the Ogatas' tragic loss — and for Blu, their uncontainable brother, whose desperate need to be loved has made him vulnerable to the most insidious of relationships. But shielding those she loves from harm is not Ivah's most difficult struggle, when she knows in her heart that her only hope for a future depends upon loosening the very ties that bind her family together.

Recommended by: *People*

"*[An] eye-opener ... A touching tale of a family's disintegration in spite of their love for one another.*"

Author Biography

Lois-Ann Yamanaka writes in the lyrical pidgin spoken by the descendents of the contract laborers who worked the sugar plantations of Hawaii. She is the author of the poetry collection, *Saturday Night at the Pahala Theatre*, and *Wild Meat and the Bully Burgers*, a novel. Born on the island of Moloka'I, she currently lives in a valley near Honolulu with her husband, son, and three dogs.

Topics to Consider

1. The jacket cover copy calls the author's use of the pidgin dialect "lyrical". Do you agree with this description? How do you think Yamanaka uses vocabulary and cultural references to emphasize her themes?

2. How do you explain the author's choice of title for her book?

3. Although she is dead, what role does Mama continue to play in the family? How would the children and Poppy's lives have differed if she had lived?

4. What sense of family do the Ogatas have? Is there love? If so, how do they express it?

5. What lessons do the Ogata children learn? What values?

6. The author grew up with animals. Why do you suppose her book is filled with stories of cruelty to animals?

7. What is the symbolic role of food in the lives of the Ogatas?

8. As the oldest girl, is Ivah a responsible surrogate mother for Blu and Maisie?

9. What motivates the individual characters in the story? Do the scenes of vulgarity and sexuality illuminate the motivations? If not, why are those scenes there?

10. What do you feel toward the characters in this book?

THE CAGE

Author: Audrey Schulman
Publisher: Avon Books
Website: www.AvonBooks.com
Available in:
Paperback, 228 pages. $10.00
(ISBN 0-380-72970-9)
Genre: Fiction

Summary

Beryl, a young photographer who specializes in animals, is hired by a magazine to join an expedition to the northern reaches of Canada to take pictures of polar bears. The three other members of the expedition are all men. The team is to live out on the tundra in a custom-equipped bus, but things go wrong, almost from the start. Before even setting out from town, Beryl gets lost in a blizzard and suffers severe frostbite. The cold causes unforeseen problems with cameras and film, and the bus is immobilized by the bears' gnawing hunger. The expedition ultimately turns into a struggle for survival, unresolved until the very last pages.

Recommended by: *Philadelphia Inquirer*

"... compelling to the last page ... symbol-studded and rich in metaphor, an allegorical tale of spiritual as well as physical survival."

Author Biography

When Audrey Schulman is not traveling the globe in search of adventure, she writes fiction, designs software, and teaches creative writing. Born in Montreal, she now lives in Boston, Massachusetts, with a small land carnivore, her cat.

Topics to Consider

1. Discuss Beryl's relationship with her mother, and how it might have affected her decision to accept an assignment like this one. Would either have wanted their relationship to be any different?

2. Brief "snapshots" of Beryl's life are interspersed throughout the first few chapters. How do they help make sense of why it is that Beryl "liked the world better through the eye of her camera?"

3. How did Beryl's vision of "ideal femininity" (p. 25) change over time?

4. A brush with death — her car spinning wildly out of control — seemed to erase Beryl's harshest fears. Do you think that it takes such an extreme experience to change one's view of the world?

5. After first meeting David and Butler, Beryl felt responsible for breaking the silence between them, and asks how they'd gotten into the field. What do you imagine Beryl would have answered had she been asked the same question in return?

6. Beryl tells Maggie, "I want to learn to survive on my own, to face extremes. I won't have really lived otherwise." Discuss ways in which you can or cannot relate to Beryl's feeling.

7. After learning about Beryl's history of relationships with men, did your feelings about her change at all? If so, in what way?

8. State-of-the-art, high-tech clothing was laughable to Jean-Claude (p. 117). What does this example have to say about the relationship between style and function?

9. Butler and Jean-Claude disagree about the best route to safety (p. 194). Given the circumstances, would you have sided with Butler and taken the risk? Could anything have been done to dissuade Butler?

10. Discuss the novel's ending. Was it satisfying? What else might you have wanted to learn about Beryl's life? Given her experience, what do you imagine her future to have looked like?

11. After reading the author's biography, what do you imagine her greatest adventure to have been like?

12. What do you think accounts for the surging popularity of "extreme sports" and "adventure travel?"

CRACKING INDIA

Author: Bapsi Sidhwa
Publisher: Milkweed Editions, 1991
Website: www.milkweed.org
Available in:
Paperback, 289 pages. $14.95
(ISBN 0-915943-56-5)
Genre: Fiction

Summary

Cracking India is a book of many voices, poignant, humorous, and desperate. It is a tale of upheaval in which every friend and enemy will be displaced. Eight-year-old Lenny, the spirited and imaginative daughter of an affluent Parsee family, narrates the story of the cracking of India during the 1940s, as she witnesses Muslims, Hindus, Christians, Parsees, and Sikhs fight for their land and their lives. As rumors of riots, fires, and massacres in distant cities become a reality, Lenny's tale follows the course of her quickly shifting life.

Recommended by: *USA Today*

"...Illustrates the power of good fiction: a historical tragedy comes alive, yielding insight into both the past and the subcontinent's turbulent present."

Author Biography

Bapsi Sidhwa is a distinguished international writer. Her other novels are *An American Brat*, *The Bride*, and *The Crow Eaters*. Among her many honors is the Lila Wallace/Readers Digest Writers Award. *Cracking India*, a *New York Times* Notable Book of the Year, has been made into the film *Earth* by noted director Deepa Mehta.

Topics to Consider

1. Do you, like Lenny, eventually feel pity for the Ice-Candy-Man? Why of why not? Do you think he truly loves Ayah or is he simply obsessed with something that he cannot attain? Why do you think he lets the mob abduct her?

2. How would this story be different if told from an adult's perspective instead of a child's? Does the full horror of the events during the Partition of Pakistan and India come across more, or less, when seen through Lenny's eyes?

3. Lenny refers to people in the story by their title — Godmother, Slavesister, Ayah, Ice-Candy-Man — she does not use their given names. How does that affect your perception of these characters?

4. What political issues were you aware of at age eight? How did you perceive different religions and their conflicts with each other?

5. What are the similarities between the massacres during the Partition of Pakistan and India and the Holocaust in Germany and Poland during World War II? What are the differences?

6. Lenny does not have the guile to lie and betrays her closest friend. At age eight, would you have known to lie to someone whom you'd known and trusted, to protect your loved ones? Do you think Lenny feels responsible for what happens to Ayah?

7. Gandhi makes an appearance in the book. Is the image of him given in the story the same as what you've learned of him from history books and in the news?

8. There is still antipathy between Pakistan and India. Do you think the conflict will ever be resolved? Why or why not?

CREEKER
A Woman's Journey

Author: Linda Scott DeRosier
Publisher: University Press of Kentucky
Website: www.uky.edu/UniversityPress/
Available in:
Hardcover, 272 pages. $27.50
(ISBN 0-8131-2123-X)
Genre: Nonfiction/Memoir/Women's Studies

Summary

Linda Sue Preston was born on a feather bed in the upper room of her Grandma Emmy's log house in the mountains of eastern Kentucky. She says that she was probably ten or eleven before she ever saw a stranger, hers was such a close-knit world. Growing up in Appalachia, she discovered the importance of family and friends, and the profound strength of the support system they created. The solid foundation built during her childhood has allowed her to conquer new frontiers in the world of academia, and in the pursuit of love. By drawing on the lessons learned in her youth, the curious Linda Sue Preston was able to become the satisfied Linda Scott DeRosier. Her story includes some hardships and failings, but through it all, DeRosier never loses sight of the importance of her heritage.

Recommended by: Kirkus Reviews

"... Her journey has been as long as, and perhaps even more unlikely than, that of the 'Coal Miner's Daughter' ... there is nothing typical about this memoir."

Author Biography

Linda Scott DeRosier, who received a Ph.D. at the University of Kentucky and an Ed.M. at Harvard University, is a professor of psychology at Rocky Mountain College in Billings, Montana.

Topics to Consider

1. Describe the status of gender relations in the Appalachia of DeRosier's childhood. Do you think that these roles were unusual for their time?

2. What do you think it means to be from Appalachia? Do you feel that those who live in this area are inherently linked?

3. As an "outsider," what words would you use to describe the town of Two-Mile? Do you think that it changed as Linda Sue did?

4. How does DeRosier's perception of wealth and its importance change throughout the work? When she was young do you think she realized she was poor?

5. Do you think that this book will change the ways that people regard the Appalachian region and its inhabitants?

6. How does the concept of "home" change throughout the work?

7. Do you agree with Linda's explanation that "education, if it takes, changes the insides of our heads so that we do not see the same world we previously saw"? Can you apply it to a particular class or experience in your own educational background?

8. Do you think that Linda's dissatisfaction with "life on the 18th green" is what really led to the breakup of her marriage? What was lacking between her and Brett?

9. Linda refers to herself as a clone of her mother. Based on what we know of these characters, do you agree with this assertion? How do you see their relationship change?

10. What was the significance of Linda Sue changing her name to Lee? What do you think changed within her that allowed her to go back to her original name?

11. DeRosier says that those that move out of the Appalachian region often feel "guilt or emptiness" for not staying at home. How do you think that her feelings about leaving her birthplace affected her life?

12. How much of Linda Sue Preston is retained by the end of this memoir? Has life outside of Appalachia greatly altered her fundamental beliefs?

DREAMING UNDER A TON OF LIZARDS

Author: Marian Michener
Publisher: Spinsters Ink, 1999
Website: www.spinsters-ink.com
Available in:
Paperback, 192 pages. $12.00
(ISBN 1-883523-34-6)
Genre: Fiction

Summary

Dreaming Under a Ton of Lizards catapults us into the lethal world of alcohol addiction. Olivia is a lesbian, a would-be writer, and an alcoholic. We see Olivia stumbling through life in a drunken stupor, obsessed with Sister Wine, the "seductive woman in green." Sister Wine fills Olivia's days with temptation, blurs the sharp edges of her life experiences, shares her nights, and haunts even her dreams. Taking her first baby steps towards sobriety, Olivia pulls away from a destructive relationship with her equally hard-drinking lover, Brooke, and retreats to an isolated cottage on the rainswept Oregon coast to concentrate on her writing. While making her first serious attempts both at penning a novel and coming to grips with her addiction, Olivia recalls her introduction to Sister Wine and the subsequent impact upon her life. Though Olivia fails in her writing, she succeeds in creating a new life for herself by finally setting out on the road to sobriety.

Recommended by: Publishers Weekly

"... The sincere, sensitive exploration of alcoholism and lesbian life merges with a genuine love story that will find grateful readers."

Author Biography

Marian Michener has an MA in Creative Writing from San Francisco State University. Her short stories and excerpts from her novel appear in various anthologies and periodicals. Ms. Michener lives in Seattle, and has been clean and sober since 1981.

Topics to Consider

1. Olivia is afraid to be alone. What causes this fear? How does she overcome it?

2. Rachel asks whether Olivia controls the alcohol or the alcohol controls Olivia. Why is it so hard for Olivia to answer?

3. How is Olivia's alcoholism intertwined with her sexuality? What impact, if any, does her relationship with Judith have upon her descent into alcohol addiction?

4. Olivia dreams of a woman in a green dress. Who is this woman? What does the green imagery represent?

5. How have the people in Olivia's life — her family, her friends, Malcolm, her lovers — shaped her into who she is today?

6. Why does Olivia contact Rachel the last time?

7. Olivia's dreams while drinking involve "dreaming under a ton of lizards" and having to evolve. What do Olivia's dreams represent? How do her dreams evolve after she stops drinking?

8. Olivia says, "I wondered what it would be like if every moment was a matter of life and death. And then I saw that it is. That every moment not paying attention is a moment dead." Is that true? Why or why not?

9. "Half the reason I drank all those years was because I was so thirsty." What does Olivia mean by these words?

10. What makes Olivia finally quit drinking for good? What gives her the strength to maintain her sobriety?

EAST OF THE MOUNTAINS

Author: David Guterson
Publisher: Harcourt Inc., 2000
Website: www.harcourt.com
Available in:
Paperback, 304 pages. $14.00
(ISBN 0-15-601104-2)
Genre: Fiction

Summary

Ben Givens, recently widowed, is a retired heart surgeon, once admired for his steadiness of hand, his precision, his endurance. He has terminal colon cancer. While Ben does not readily accept defeat, he is determined to avoid suffering rather than engage it. And so, accompanied by his two hunting dogs, he sets out on his last hunt. The main issues for Ben as a doctor had been tactical and so it would be with his death. But he hadn't considered the persuasiveness of memory, or life's mystery. Just when he thinks there is no turning back on his journey, nothing to lose that wasn't lost, his power of intervention is called upon and his very identity tested.

Recommended by: *Time*

"... Best read, perhaps, as a kind of firelit Steinbeck western about how a deliberate man learns the virtues of having his plans overturned and comes to embrace the life he'd all but given up on."

Author Biography

In addition to his best-selling novel, *Snow Falling on Cedars*, David Guterson is the author of a collection of short stories, *The Country Ahead of Us, the Country Behind*, and of *Family Matters: Why Home Schooling Makes Sense*. He has won the PEN/Faulkner Award and an ABBY Award. He lives in Washington state.

Topics to Consider

1. What is the significance of Ben's movement eastward?

2. Do you think that coincidence and chance occur too often in the novel? What is the significance of the several references to miracles?

3. If "Suicide was at odds with the life he knew, at odds with all he understood, of himself and of the world," why does Ben plan such a carefully thought-out, staged suicide? Given Ben's views on death and dying, why does he want to end his life in this "cradle of apple orchards"?

4. What bearing on Ben's present does each of his memories have? How do those memories help us understand Ben's life and behavior?

5. Why does Guterson pay so much attention to details of landscape and natural phenomena? How is Guterson's presentation of each landscape important in terms of the corresponding stage in Ben's life and of his view of life at each stage?

6. What role does hunting play in Ben's life? In what ways does his attitude toward hunting change?

7. As he settles Rex into the cab of Stu Robinson's tractor-trailer, Ben thinks, "There were no good answers to important questions." What are the important questions, from Ben's perspective? What answers does he find? Which of those answers, if any, are "good"?

8. What is the importance of Ben's experience in the field hospital in Italy, and of Ben's memory of that experience? What influence did the Army surgeon have on Ben?

9. In what ways might Ben be compared to Job and Don Quixote? What other biblical and literary references occur, and what is their relevance?

ENEMY OF THE AVERAGE

Author: Margaret Nicol
Publisher: Allen A. Knoll, 1999
Available in:
Hardcover, 618 pages. $25.00
(ISBN 1-888310-60-X)
Genre: Fiction/Roman à clef

Summary

Hanna Mazurka was the Enemy of the Average. Born Zdenka Oleska on a poor Polish farm, she was one of the most astonishing women of her time. She left home a disgruntled teenager, unsophisticated and minimally educated. With her stunning beauty, ambition and cunning she grew to marry and control six of the world's richest, most accomplished men. Aristocrat, lover, ersatz opera diva, adulterer, enigma and creator of a world-class eclectic garden, Hanna Mazurka's life was one of opulence, spectacle and heartbreaks. An extraordinary novel spanning more than a century, *Enemy of the Average* abounds with magnetic and memorable characters.

Recommended by: Robert Lindsey, author, *The Falcon and the Snowman*

"... *A beautifully written, Byzantine tale of money, sex, music and the velvet-gloved, ruthless ambition of a remarkable woman. What's even more amazing is that it is rooted in fact.*"

Author Biography

Margaret Nicol is an opera buff and an avid gardener. She has limited herself to one husband. They live in the hills of Santa Barbara, California in an empty nest.

Topics to Consider

1. How did you feel about Hanna Mazurka? Was she an ambitious feminist or a selfish opportunist?
2. Where do you think truth leaves off and fiction begins in this story?
3. Why do you think she pursued her "singing career" with such determination in the face of failure? What did it do for her?
4. What is your assessment of the husbands? What did they see in her? Why did they give her so much for so little in return?
5. Did she love any of them or did they love her?
6. How does her life reflect the status of women in the first half of this century?
7. How much do the circumstances of history play a part in how Hanna Mazurka's life unfolds? (Two world wars, the fall of the Russian czars, etc.)

EVENING

Author: Susan Minot
Publisher: Vintage Books, 1999
Website: www.vintagebooks.com/read
Available in:
Paperback, 288 pages. $12.00
(ISBN 0-375-70026-9)
Genre: Fiction

Summary

Ann Lord is dying of cancer. As she lies in bed, drifting in and out of consciousness, visited by friends and family members, we enter the twilight world of her memories, dreams, and regrets. Although she has had three husbands and five children, it is, above all, to one turbulent weekend that her mind keeps returning — and to one all-too-brief, never-to-be-forgotten romance. As she loses hold on present reality, Ann is drawn insistently back forty years to memories of the glorious Maine wedding of her friend Lila, where she met, fell in love with, and finally lost the one man who has ever meant anything to her; and where a fateful tragedy struck at the heart of their happy group of friends.

Recommended by: *The New York Times Book Review*

"In spare and lovely language, Susan Minot has set forth a real life, in all its particularity and splendor and pain. This is the task of the novelist, and Minot has succeeded admirably."

Author Biography

Susan Minot grew up in Manchester-by-the-Sea. Her first novel, *Monkeys*, was published in a dozen countries and received the Prix Fémina Étranger in France. She is the author of *Lust and Other Stories* and *Folly*, a novel, and she wrote the screenplay for Bernardo Bertolucci's *Stealing Beauty*.

Topics to Consider

1. Minot renders Ann's thoughts in what might be called stream-of-consciousness. Which things does Ann remember most distinctly? Which does she remember least distinctly? Which does she repress? What does the relative weight she allows each memory tell us about the emotional shape of her life?

2. Outsiders see Ann rather differently than she sees herself. What, if anything, does this elderly Ann have in common with the young, passionate Ann she still feels herself to be? What does this dichotomy imply about the differences between our inner selves and the outer person our friends and family see?

3. What might have attracted Ann to each of her three husbands? How did she come to view each of them as the years went by? How does the language in which Ann recalls her marriages differ from the language in which she recalls Harris, and what does this difference in language tell us about her feelings?

4. How would you describe each of Ann's children? How has each been molded and shaped by his or her relationship with her? How does each of them behave toward her? Has the essential sadness of Ann's life rubbed off on them?

5. What sort of a person is Harris, really? What do you deduce about him and about his feelings, principles, and desires from his behavior, from what others say about him?

6. Does Ann ever feel responsible for what happened to Buddy? Does Harris? Does a sense of responsibility for this tragedy, or a lack of one, have any specific effect on Ann's future life?

7. Ann conducts a number of imagined conversations with Harris in which the two meet again, for the first time in forty years. What sort of person is this elderly, imaginary Harris? Is he the sort of character you can imagine the young Harris growing into? How do you think the real sixty-five-year-old Harris might remember Ann?

8. If Ann and Harris had married, what sort of a life might they have had? Would they have been happy together? Might Ann have been unhappy and unfulfilled even with Harris?

FALLING LEAVES
The Memoir of an Unwanted Chinese Daughter

Author: Adeline Yen Mah
Publisher: Broadway Books, 1999
Website: www.randomhouse.com
Available in:
Paperback, 304 pages. $13.00
(ISBN 0-7679-0357-9)
Genre: Nonfiction/Memoir

Summary

Adeline Yen Mah's years of mental and physical abuse began when her mother died shortly after giving birth to her, leaving Adeline to suffer under a cold and manipulative stepmother whose sadistic acts were never questioned by her husband. Adeline's only refuge was her beloved Aunt Baba, a remarkable woman who rebelled against traditional Chinese custom, and lavished encouragement and affection on her niece. Eventually, Adeline traveled to London to study medicine, then made a new life for herself in the U.S. But her horrific childhood continued to haunt her, until at last she was able to examine and accept her roots.

Recommended by: Amy Tan, author of *The Joy Luck Club*

"Riveting. A marvel of memory. Poignant proof of the human will to endure."

Author Biography

Adeline Yen Mah is a physician and writer. She lives in Huntington Beach, California. *Falling Leaves* is her first book. Recently she completed her second, a book for children entitled *Chinese Cinderella*. Adeline is dedicating both books to unwanted children in the hope that they will persist to do their best in the face of despair, to believe that in the end their spirit will prevail.

Topics to Consider

1. Why do you think the author chose the reading of her father's will as the point in time to start her story?

2. Overall how would you characterize the author's life in China? Was there any happiness for her? What strategies does she use to cope with the situation and who aided her in those efforts? How would you have reacted in similar circumstances?

3. Discuss the social hierarchy of the Yen household. How did Adeline fit in? How about Ye Ye and Aunt Baba?

4. Of the many instances of cruelty that Adeline faced as a child, which ones affected you most strongly? Why?

5. How would you characterize the author's relationship with her Aunt Baba? How about with her grandfather Ye Ye?

6. How did the author's life change once she moved to England? What factors motivated this change? Why was medical school such an appropriate place for her?

7. During her time in America the author's relationship with her parents and her siblings changes. Discuss these changes and what brought them about.

8. Adeline is possessed of remarkable strength, resilience, and compassion. Is there any precedent for this in her family?

9. The author manages to succeed and ultimately leads a happy life. How is she able to achieve this despite her childhood emotional deprivation?

10. Memoirs centered on unhappy childhoods, such as *Angela's Ashes*, are increasingly popular. Why do you think this is so? How have these memoirs influenced modern storytelling?

FINAL STORM

Author: Lewis R. Walton
Publisher: Aralon Press, 1999
Available in:
Paperback, 224 pages. $7.95
(ISBN 0-9656834-1-9)
Genre: Fiction

Summary

The Dow was at an all-time high. The world was at peace. Then a series of crises left people jobless and frightened, their cities endangered by urban terrorism. As President Barton let a war break out just to save his political life, religious zealots took over: thinking that religion might ward off calamity, they tried to force a national moral revival. But buried in their plan was a risk: what if their good intentions were hijacked by an unseen foe with a hidden agenda? *Final Storm* is an adventure story of religion and politics, with a tantalizing suggestion of the supernatural.

Recommended by: Dr. Herbert Douglass

"Walton has done it again! Not only is Final Storm *the most powerful of current futuristic scenarios, it captures the heart as well as the head — it grabs both like glue."*

Author Biography

Lewis R. Walton is a former newscaster who reported such stories as the Cuban Missile Crisis and the assassination of John F. Kennedy. He holds a Juris Doctorate, magna cum laude, and has earned academic awards in literary and constitutional law. His book *The Lucifer Diary* has been optioned for a feature film.

Topics to Consider

1. President Gregory Barton was, at best, a talented politician who could dazzle you at the piano and charm you with his line of gab — while letting a war happen just to save his job. What turned him into someone who would walk away from the White House over an issue of principle?

2. For decades we've gotten hints — some of them frivolous, some of them too credible to ignore — that there may be an intelligent force beyond the realm of our five senses. Is there a possibility that something (or someone) really is "out there?"

3. If the answer to #2 is yes, then who (or what) is it? And what does it want?

4. Max Marple is an irreverent CIA specialist who engineers the disappearance of a president and then rides off, on a Harley, toward the sanctuary of Mexico. He is motivated by adventure, not idealism, yet he places his life on the line for an ideal he may not care about. In this allegory, whom does he represent?

5. And President Barton, the naughty kid turned idealist — whom does *he* represent?

6. "Don't it always seem to go, that you don't know what you've got 'til it's gone." Could the lyrics of a '60s song apply to such intangibles as human rights? Or the Constitution? Or the soul of a nation?

7. What do you think of a woman who, just hours after learning that she has been deeply wronged by her husband, accompanies him into the nightmare of flight from an angry country?

8. If some unseen intelligence shares our space and time without revealing itself to our senses, wouldn't it have to be smarter and stronger than we?

9. Tabloids often predict apocalypse. But could the world really enter a terminal crisis? And if so, might unseen forces intervene?

FINDING GRACE

Author: Mary Saracino
Publisher: Spinsters Ink, 1999
Website: www.spinsters-ink.com
Available in:
Paperback, 288 pages. $12.00
(ISBN 1-883523-33-8)
Genre: Fiction

Summary

Eleven-year-old Peanut Giovanni describes the explosive aftermath of her mother's decision to take her three young daughters and run away with her lover, a priest — leaving her home, her marriage, and her two teenage sons behind. From the beginning, it is clear to Peanut that her mother has made a terrible mistake. The happy family Marie Giovanni had hoped to create with Patrick and her three daughters does not materialize. Instead, tragedy strikes the Giovanni family, undermining the already turbulent relationship between Marie and Patrick. Seeking to escape the turmoil and to be reunited with her father, Peanut, instead, finds Grace. Memories of Grace later give Peanut the strength to protect herself from her mother's life choices and to forge her own identity as Regina Giovanni.

Recommended by: *Booklist*

"... a compelling account of grace and redemption from alcohol abuse, poverty, domestic violence, and other aspects of family tragedy."

Author Biography

Mary Saracino is a native of Seneca Falls, NY. Her first novel, *No Matter What*, was published by Spinsters Ink in 1993 and was a 1994 Minnesota Book Award finalist in the fiction category. Ms. Saracino's work has appeared in a variety of literary magazines and anthologies, including *Sinister Wisdom*, *Voices in Italian Americana*, and *Italian Americana*. Ms. Saracino lives in Denver, Colorado.

Topics to Consider

1. What is the meaning of the title *Finding Grace*?
2. Peanut appears to accept Joey's death without questioning how he died. What is ironic about Joey's death?
3. Why is Grace afraid to contact the authorities after she finds Peanut and Rosa? Is her fear justified?
4. When Peanut and Rosa decide to return to their mother, they lie to protect Grace; Grace agrees to their cover-up. Is this appropriate? Can you think of any other situations where a lie is justified?
5. When Peanut's mother tells her they are never going back to Pisa, Peanut appears content with this statement and even comforts her mother. Why?
6. This story takes place during the Vietnam War. Is this significant? Why or why not?
7. Peanut becomes more assertive after her stay with Grace. Why?
8. Peanut drops her nickname during her stay with Grace. What is the significance of this action?
9. What does Uncle Tony give Peanut? What is the significance of this item?
10. Peanut often refers to "swallowing air" or "not having enough air." What is the significance of this imagery?
11. How does Peanut's relationship with her mother change between the beginning of the novel and its conclusion?

GARDENS IN THE DUNES

Author: Leslie Marmon Silko

Publisher: Scribner Paperback Fiction, (4/00)

Website: www.SimonSays.com

Available in:
Paperback, 480 pages. $14.00
(ISBN 0-684-86332-4)

Genre: Fiction

Summary

When white soldiers destroy her home and her family, Indigo is taken from her tribe, placed in a school designed to give Indian children a European-American education, and eventually adopted by a proper Victorian couple. Although her parents are loving, Indigo cannot forget her past or forsake the centuries-old wisdom of her people and fully embrace the Christian virtues that shape her parents' lives. Over the years, Indigo's spirit and strength profoundly affects the lives and beliefs of all three members of the closely-knit family. The author eloquently portrays the clash between the Native American spirit and the values — and hypocrisies — of white upper-class society, and creates a memorable heroine who learns how to honor the best of both cultures.

Recommended by: Melissa Levine, *The San Francisco Chronicle*

"... More accurately reminiscent of Joseph Conrad ... a rich descendent well worth reading."

Author Biography

Leslie Marmon Silko, a former Professor of English and Fiction Writing, is the author of many award-winning novels, short stories, and essays. She lives in Tucson, Arizona.

Topics to Consider

1. Do you consider this to be a feminist novel, or simply one that features strong female characters? Is there a difference between the two?

2. What does this book suggest about the importance of mothers and mothering?

3. How do you feel about the author's portrayal of men?

4. What does the book say about the dangers of materialism and the consequences of putting a price on natural treasures?

5. Compare Indigo's spiritual, survivalist relationship to nature with Edward's scientific, capitalist approach. Does the book suggest that one is more ethical than the other?

6. Contrast the Indians' yearly Ghost Dance with the annual Masque of the Blue Garden hosted by Hattie's sister-in-law. What do these gatherings reveal about the values, beliefs, and lifestyles of their participants?

7. Compare and contrast the book's depictions of the affluence of high society and the abundant riches of nature. Do you find it a happy or sad moment when Indigo trades her fancy new dresses for food at the end of the novel?

8. How do the challenges Indigo faces among the Sand Lizards differ from those she encounters during her travels with Hattie and Edward?

9. Discuss the role of the supernatural in the narrative and in the lives of the characters. How does the book explore the interplay of religion, mysticism, and spirituality?

10. In the end, what do Hattie and Indigo gain from each other? To what degree do they influence one another? Which of them has been more profoundly changed by the end of their journey?

THE GIANT'S HOUSE

Author: Elizabeth McKracken
Publisher: Bard Books (Avon), 1998
Website: www.AvonBooks.com/Bard
Available in:
Paperback, 290 pages. $12.50
(ISBN 0-380-73020-0)
Genre: Fiction

Summary

The year is 1950, and in a small town on Cape Cod twenty-six-year-old librarian Peggy Cort feels like love and life have stood her up. Until the day James Carlson Sweatt — the "over-tall" eleven-year-old boy who's talk of the town — walks into her library and changes her life forever. Two misfits whose lonely paths cross at the circulation desk, Peggy and James are odd candidates for friendship, but nevertheless they find their lives entwined in ways that neither one could have predicted. And as James grows — six foot five at age twelve, then seven feet, then eight — so does Peggy's heart and their most singular romance.

Recommended by: Dorothy Allison, Author

"This book is my kind of romance — fated and complicated, with a heroine who is as difficult as I could want ... a woman who wins you over with the audacity of her obsessions."

Author Biography

Elizabeth McCracken is the author of the ALA Notable story collection *Here's Your Hat What's Your Hurry*. In 1996, she was named one of the Best Young American Novelists by *Granta* magazine. She lives in Massachusetts, where, until recently, she was a full-time librarian. *The Giant's House* was a finalist for the 1996 National Book Award in fiction.

Topics to Consider

1 Do you think that Peggy's perception of librarians as the sort of occupation that others assume attracts "a certain deformed personality" (p. 9) is true? Do you think her character fits that assessment?

2 What is it about James's personal circumstances that makes magic seem so attractive to him? What makes him, later on, long to be a lawyer, to leave Massachusetts?

3 Can you picture Peggy making choices concerning her life other than those she makes (e.g. being a librarian, moving to Brewsterville)? Does she view herself as having other options?

4 What do you imagine has happened to transform Peggy from the self-described socially adept girl she was growing up to be into the misfit we see her to be later?

5 Consider giants and dwarves. In a society that places a premium on being like everybody else, what would it be like to be a member of, as Peggy puts it, "a solitary race"? (p. 61)

6 Do you think, like Peggy, that the existence of James proves God's existence? Or, like James himself, that it disproves it?

7 Peggy finally comes to believe that people choose to be in love rather than falling. Do you agree, with her and James, that someone can choose not to experience unrequited love?

8 When are people who have an extraordinary medical condition like James's better off — when people try to treat them just like everybody else or when they fully acknowledge the difference that sets them apart?

9 Compare Patty Flood's idea of being smart and sad vs. dumb and happy. Which is preferable?

10 Would James have been a happy person were it not for the unavoidable circumstance of his height?

11 How might things have gone differently for Peggy had she revealed the true identity of Dotty's father?

GOODNIGHT, NEBRASKA

Author: Tom McNeal
Publisher: Vintage Books, 1999
Website: www.vintagebooks.com/read
Available in:
Paperback, 336 pages. $12.00
(ISBN 0-375-70429-9)
Genre: Fiction

Summary

When seventeen-year-old Randall Hunsacker arrives in the Great Plains town of Goodnight, Nebraska, pop. 1680, it is with the knowledge that here he has a second chance. Here he can escape violent events back home in Salt Lake City and build a new life for himself. But starting from scratch proves to be far more problematic than he had hoped, and he soon realizes that the picture-perfect farm town into which he is absorbed conceals lives that are as complex, troubled, and lonely as lives are throughout the world. *Goodnight, Nebraska* describes Randall's ten-year progress, from disreputable friends and a too-early marriage to a renewed effort and, at last, a possibility for the sort of redemption he has long been seeking.

Recommended by: *The Denver Post*

"A remarkable debut! ... Vivid and alive."

Author Biography

Tom McNeal had always been fascinated by his mother's stories of her girlhood in a remote Nebraska town, and knew that he eventually wanted to write about this region. He therefore spent several years in Hay Springs, Nebraska, a town even smaller than the fictional Goodnight. First published in 1998, this is his first novel. Tom McNeal is married and now lives in Fallbrook, California.

Topics to Consider

1. How and when was the pattern set for Louise's wild and self-destructive life? Why is she unable to break out of this pattern, while Randall, ultimately, is?

2. How does Randall's experience with Anna Belknap pave the way for his attraction to Marcy? What does Randall look for in a girl? How does he define love, and how does he modify this definition as he grows up?

3. Was Randall's staged accident in Salt Lake City a deliberate suicide attempt? If not, what might he have been trying to bring about? How does this car accident parallel and echo the car accident at the end of the novel?

4. Why does Randall behave in such a self-destructive fashion for so many years, even though he clearly craves love and acceptance? What unresolved issues in his past contribute to this behavior?

5. As a reader, how do your feelings toward Lewis change and develop as the novel progresses? Who has a more practical philosophy of life, Lewis or Dorothy? Which proves more resilient in the end?

6. What sort of statement does this book make about small-town life? Does life in Goodnight seem impossibly claustrophobic, or is it attractive? What must one give up to live in a place like Goodnight, and what does one gain?

7. Randall and Marcy both hope to "start over." What do their experiences tell us about starting over? Is it ever really possible to do so?

8. How do patterns of behavior, of love and marriage, of achievement, repeat themselves from generation to generation among characters in this novel? How do parents' mistakes and decisions affect the decisions their children will eventually make?

9. Do you believe that a place or a community molds its inhabitants in its own image? If so, how would you describe Goodnight and its citizens?

THE HOURS

Author: Michael Cunnigham

Publisher: Picador USA, 2000

Website: www.stmartins.com

Available in:
Paperback, 229 pages. $13.00
(ISBN 0-312-24302-2)

Genre: Fiction

Summary

Clarissa Vaughan, a book editor in present-day Greenwich Village, is organizing a party for her oldest friend, Richard, and AIDS-stricken poet who has just won a major literary prize. Laura Brown, a young wife and mother in 1949 Los Angeles, cares for her toddler and prepares a birthday cake for her husband as she tries to resist increasing waves of panic and feelings of alienation from her humdrum yet demanding life. And Virginia Woolf herself, the third woman, works on her new novel, *Mrs. Dalloway*, chats with her husband and sister, bickers with her cook, and attempts to come to terms with her longings for escape and even for death. As the novel jump-cuts through the century, the lives and stories of the three women converge the night of Clarissa's party for Richard.

Recommended by: *USA Today*

"A smashing tour de force and an utterly invigorating experience. If this book does not make you jump up from the sofa, looking at life and literature in new ways, check to see if you have a pulse."

Author Biography

Michael Cunningham's novel *A Home at the End of the World* was published to acclaim in 1990. His novel *Flesh and Blood* was published in 1995, and that year he won a Whiting Writer's Award. *The Hours*, Cunningham's third novel, received the 1999 Pulitzer Prize for Fiction and the PEN/Faulkner Award.

Topics to Consider

1. Clarissa Vaughan is described as an ordinary woman. Do you accept this valuation? If so, what does it imply about being ordinary? What makes someone, by contrast, extraordinary?

2. What does the novel imply about the fine line between sanity and insanity? Would you classify Richard as insane? How does his mental state compare with that of Virginia? Of Laura as a young wife?

3. Each of the novel's three principal women occasionally feels a sense of detachment, of playing a role. Is role-playing an essential part of living in the world, and of behaving sanely?

4. What does this book tell us about the creative process? How does each character revise and improve his or her creation during the course of the story?

5. Which characters keep their inner selves ruthlessly separate from their outer ones? Why?

6. Each of the novel's characters sees himself or herself, most of the time, as a failure. Are such feelings an essential and inevitable part of the human condition?

7. What does the novel and its characters have to say about the transition from youth to middle-age? Should such passages be resisted or embraced?

8. Which of the characters loves the idea of death, as others love life? What makes some decide to die, others to live?

9. If you have read Virginia Woolf's *Mrs. Dalloway*, would you describe *The Hours* as a modern version of it? A commentary upon it? A dialogue with it? Which characters in *The Hours* correspond with those of Woolf's novel?

HUMMINGBIRD HOUSE

Author: Patricia Henley
Publisher: MacMurray and Beck (5/00)
Website: www.macmurraybeck.com
Available in:
Paperback, 300 pages. $13.00
(ISBN 1-878448-98-6)
Genre: Fiction

Summary

When Kate Banner, an American midwife in Nicaragua, loses another patient — a young woman who had given birth only the night before on the bottom of a swamped wooden boat — she knows it is time to go home. Because to care for the children of war, you have to cut off pieces of your heart. But traveling home leads her to Guatemala, where even children sometimes disappear. This is the story of a woman's struggles to face new territories of love and war in the middle of her life — a moving and emotionally trustworthy tale of a human heart unbinding itself in the most unjust of worlds.

Recommended by: John Sayles

"... A strong, deeply felt novel ... A heart-breaking book."

Author Biography

Patricia Henley spent five months traveling in Central America and southern Mexico while writing *Hummingbird House*. She has published two collections of stories, *Friday Night at Silver Star* and *The Secret of Cartwheels* and a book of poems, *Back Roads*. Her stories have been anthologized in *Best American Short Stories* and *The Pushcart Prize Anthology*. She teaches in the MFA Creative Writing program at Purdue. In 1999, *Hummingbird House* was a National Book Award Finalist and *New Yorker* Fiction Prize Finalist.

Topics to Consider

1. What is the single action without which this novel could not have taken place?

2. The political realities of this war in Central America could be much more present than they are. What does the author gain by this and what does she lose?

3. It seems to be Kate's pattern of behavior to create distance when her desire is the opposite. How does this affect the action of the novel?

4. What are the forms that faith takes over the course of the novel?

5. What causes Dixie to lose faith and what does he lose faith in?

6. When the novel opens, Kate's self-worth seems to be based on aid and nurturing. Does this change by the end?

7. How many maternal relationships are portrayed in this book?

8. Water imagery is fairly constant throughout the novel. What does this symbolize?

I CAPTURE THE CASTLE

Author: Dodie Smith

Publisher: Thomas Dunne Books/ St. Martin's Press, 1999

Website: www.stmartins.com

Available in:
Paperback, 352 pages. $14.95
(ISBN 0-312-20165-6)

Genre: Fiction

Summary

Seventeen-year-old Cassandra and her family live in not-so-genteel poverty in a ramshackle English castle. Here she strives, over six turbulent months, to hone her writing skills. She fills three notebooks with sharply funny yet poignant entries. Her journals candidly chronicle the great changes that take place within the old castle's walls, and her own first descent into love. By the time she pens her final entry, she has "captured the castle" – and the heart of the reader – in one of literature's most enchanting entertainments. (First published by Little, Brown & Co., 1948.)

Recommended by: J.K. Rowling, author of *Harry Potter and ...*

"This book has one of the most charismatic narrators I've ever met... Seventeen-year-old Cassandra Mortman captures the castle in her insightful, witty journal entries."

Author Biography

Dorothy Gladys "Dodie" Smith was born in 1896 in Lancashire, England. She was one of the most successful female dramatists of her generation. This, her first novel, was written when she lived in America during the '40s and marked her crossover debut from playwright to novelist. She is best known for her stories for young readers, including *The Hundred and One Dalmatians*, inspired by her own dog, Pongo. Dodie Smith died in 1990.

Topics to Consider

1. How might readers have responded differently to the novel at the time it was first published? Why does the novel continue to appeal to readers today as it did in 1948?

2. Why do you think Dodie Smith chose the form of the diary to tell the story of Cassandra and the Mortmain family?

3. Beyond a few spare descriptions, Smith tells us little about Mortmain's novel. What do you imagine *Jacob Wrestling* to be about?

4. A voracious reader, Cassandra compares her situation to that of the Bennets in Jane Austen's *Pride and Prejudice*. How would you compare the situation of the Mortmain sisters to that of the Bennet sisters?

5. Why does Mortmain encourage Cassandra to be "brisk" with Stephen? What does this book have to say about class in mid-twentieth-century England?

6. What is the meaning of the book's title?

7. What does the book say about English preconceptions of Americans and America and vice versa?

8. How does the book reflect society's changing views toward women during the first half of this century? How do the women in the novel view the roles and opportunities open to them both in the family and in the world at large differently?

9. Over the course of the novel, Cassandra comes to seem less a child "with a little green hand" and more a young woman. How is *I Capture the Castle* a story of Cassandra's coming of age?

IN SESSION
The Bond Between Women and Their Therapists

Author: Deborah A. Lott
Publisher: W.H. Freeman, 1999
Website: whfreeman.com
Available in:
Paperback (4/00), 321 pages. $14.95
(ISBN 0-7167-4025-7)
Hardcover, 321 pages. $23.95
(ISBN 0-7167-3562-8)
Genre: Nonfiction/Women's Issues

Summary

Readers of *In Session* enter the consulting room and discover that relationships between women and their therapists are similar to many of those outside the psychotherapeutic alliance: they can be complex, intimate, and even erotic. Drawing on the stories of over 300 women in therapy, interviews with leading psychotherapists and a comprehensive review of the professional literature, **Deborah Lott** found great discrepancies in what therapists state publicly about the boundaries between therapist and client and what really happens in the sanctity of their own offices.

Recommended by: Hope Edelman, author of *Mother of My Mother*

"An insightful and beautifully written book ... a fascinating read."

Author Biography

Deborah A. Lott has been a writer and editor specializing in psychology, medicine, and health for twenty years. She is a frequent contributor to *Psychiatric Times, Psychology Today*, and other consumer health publications.

Topics to Consider

1. Discuss the stigmas still surrounding therapy, medication, and mental illness. When people talk about their therapy, how are others likely to react? How would the public react to learning that a political leader was in psychotherapy?

2. Why do you suppose women today no longer suffer from the syndrome identified in Anna O.'s day as hysteria? Are some mental illnesses caused by the cultures in which they occur?

3. What are some of the consequences of being in a relationship where the power and degree of intimacy are not reciprocal? Aside from psychotherapy, what other relationships are asymmetrical?

4. Idealization of the therapist is one of the most common unrealistic assumptions women make. Are there situations in which people are more likely to idealize others, or the lives of others? Does powerlessness lead to greater idealization of the powerful?

5. What are the sources of therapists' power? How can this power be abused?

6. Discuss the role and purpose of boundaries in the therapy relationship. Are there circumstances in which boundaries are important in other personal and professional relationships?

7. In what situations (if any) do you think it's all right for therapists to touch their clients? Have you ever been in therapy with a therapist who offered hugs?

8. What evidence of transference do you see in people's daily lives? Do you think that people today are less apt to see authority figures and political leaders as parental figures than were people of past generations?

9. What do you believe is/is not possible in short-term therapy? What are the virtues/risks of a short-term model?

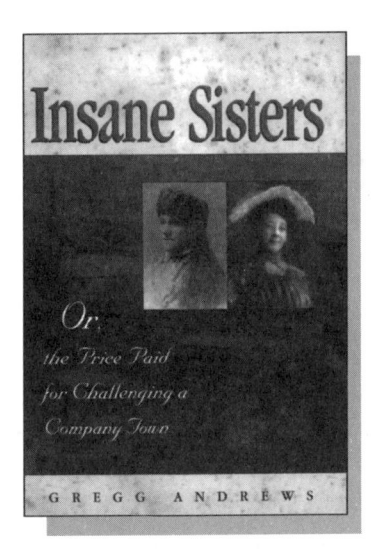

INSANE SISTERS
Or, the Price Paid for Challenging a Company Town

Author: Gregg Andrews

Publisher: University of Missouri Press, 1999

Website: www.system.missouri.edu/upress

Available in: Hardcover, 256 pages. $29.95 (ISBN 0-8262-1240-9)

Genre: Nonfiction/Women's Studies

Summary

Insane Sisters is the extraordinary tale of two sisters, Mary Alice Heinbach and Euphemia B. Koller, and their seventeen-year property dispute against the nation's leading cement corporation — the Atlas Portland Cement Company. Gregg Andrews traces the dire consequences the sisters suffered while trying to uphold their rights and provides a fascinating look at how the intersection of gender, class, and law shaped the history and politics of one small community.

Recommended by: Millie Allen Beik

"A well-written, well-researched, fascinating story of intrigue worthy of John Grisham."

Author Biography

Gregg Andrews was born in Hannibal, Missouri, and grew up in Ilasco. An Associate Professor of History at Southwest Texas State University in San Marcos, Andrews is the author of *City of Dust: A Cement Company Town in the Land of Tom Sawyer*.

Topics to Consider

1. Discuss the legal battles of Mollie Heinbach and Feemy Koller. What do their cases reveal about the legal status of women in the early twentieth century? Have times changed?

2. What is your opinion of the marriage of Mollie and Sam Heinbach? Did Mollie deserve to inherit Sam's estate? Were her attempts to gain financial independence justified by the lack of economic opportunities open to women in her era, or were they unjustified?

3. What is your opinion of Feemy Koller? How would she fare in present-day America?

4. Did Mollie or Feemy show signs of mental illness? Were the interventions of the mental health professionals appropriate or inappropriate?

5. *Insane Sisters* portrays Ilasco as a town in which those on the margins of power — immigrants, women, the poor — are virtually disenfranchised by the political and economic elites. Do you think this is an accurate portrayal, or is it biased?

6. Is Ilasco a typical American small town, or is it atypical? Are company towns such as Ilasco still with us today?

LEARNING FROM HANNAH
Secrets for a Life Worth Living

Author: William H. Thomas, M.D.

Publisher: VanderWyk & Burnham, 1999

Website: www.VandB.com

Available in:
Hardcover, 240 pages. $21.95
(ISBN 1-889242-09-8)

Genre: Fiction/Social Issues/Inspiration

Summary

Bill and Jude, a hard-working professional couple, plan a long overdue vacation. When their rented sailboat capsizes in a storm, they are violently wrenched from the life they have known; they narrowly escape death and awaken in a land called Kallimos. Fearful and angry at first, they come to trust the old woman Hannah, who is in charge of their care. From her, they learn the wisdom of Kallimos, and in time, they accept their new life. Acceptance turns to love — so strong that when they are again torn away, they suffer a spiritual breakdown. With help from Hannah, Bill tries to bring the wisdom of Kallimos into his work, only to learn that it won't be as easy as he thought.

Recommended by: *The Small Press Book Review*

"Like a fable, Learning from Hannah divulges deep truths about human nature while imparting a timeless moral message."

Author Biography

William H. Thomas is a physician in family medicine and geriatrics. He heads a consulting and advocacy group committed to improving the care received by the elderly. He has been honored by the Giraffe Project (for sticking his neck out) and has received an America's Award as an unsung hero who personifies the American character and spirit. He lives in Sherburne, NY, with his wife and children.

Topics to Consider

1. What do you think was the author's purpose for setting the book in a fantastical setting, instead of in a known or possibly recognizable society?

2. What were Bill and Jude's initial perceptions of and reactions to the people of Kallimos? How would your reactions have been similar/different?

3. Do you think you would eventually have come to accept and even love the way of life, as Bill and Jude did? What was the easiest aspect to accept, and what was the most difficult aspect?

4. The author had Bill and Jude list ten lessons they learned while on Kallimos. Do you feel the lessons are realistic? How might you implement them in your own interactions with elders? Can our society implement the lessons, do you think?

5. Which story did you like best? Why?

6. How would our society as a whole change as a result of the Eden Alternative? Would the implementation of those beliefs cause rapid or gradual change? Who would benefit the most?

7. What do you think was the point of the final story, the story about King Sarop and the building of ocean-going vessels? Why do you suppose the author did not provide the moral or lesson for that story?

8. Which principle affected you the most? Why?

9. How did you feel as you read the Epilogue, where the author talked about his own family? Why do you think the author shared this information?

10. On the page before the table of contents, the author provides this quotation from Carlyle: "All work is a seed sown; it grows and spreads, and sows itself anew." What meaning does this have for you now that you have finished the book?

LIVING ON THE EDGE
Fiction by Peace Corps Writers

Editor: John Coyne
Publisher: Curbstone Press, 1999
Website: www.curbstone.org
Available in:
Paperback, 317 pages. $17.95
(ISBN 1-880684-57-8)
Genre: Fiction/Multicultural studies

Summary

This book contains seventeen stories by Peace Corps authors writing about the Third World, including well-known authors such as John Coyne, John Givens, Norman Rush and Paul Theroux, as well as work by exciting emerging authors like Mark Jacobs and Marnie Mueller. All these stories reflect the impact the Peace Corps experience had on former volunteers who write across cultures in the literary tradition of Joseph Conrad, E. M. Forster, and Paul Bowles. A unique feature of *Living on the Edge* is that each author has included a commentary on how he or she came to write the anthologized story.

Recommended by: *Kirkus Reviews*

"For anyone interested in the U.S. and its place in the world, this collection will provide a good picture of diplomacy on a personal scale."

Author Biography

John Coyne was with the first group of Peace Corps Volunteers to Ethiopia and is the founder and editor of RPCV Writers and Readers, a newsletter for and about Peace Corps volunteers. New York City is his home town.

Topics to Consider

1. Cross-cultural writers, as Eileen Drew puts it, "see things from outside the mainstream." What examples can you find in the stories of this peculiar "angle of vision?" Do you have similar experiences of your own where you viewed a situation differently from others?

2. Why is this collection of short stories called "Living on the Edge?"

3. Discuss the role of humor in these short stories. Is it used to offset realities? To heighten them? Is it a genre in itself?

4. One reviewer noted that the stories offered instances of "deep confusion and transcendent communion." Can you offer examples? What do these stories as a whole reveal about the American character? Speculate on how some of these characters have been changed and in what ways they may react differently on re-entry into U.S. culture.

5. In *A Virgin Twice*, under which circumstances might we judge the morality or ethics of people of another culture? To what does the "virgin" of the title refer? In what ways might the story be said to be "magical"? What does the story suggest about the nature of justice?

6. Does the story *The Egg Queen Rises* seem to have a political dimension? If so, how would you describe the political issue or issues being framed?

7. Is there a "hero" in the story *Snow Man*? Is the main character an "anti-hero"? What differences do you notice between the schools in Ethiopia and the United States? What do you notice that is similar?

8. In the story *The Ones Left Behind*, why did the author tell this story from the viewpoint of the African servant? What is the message of this story?

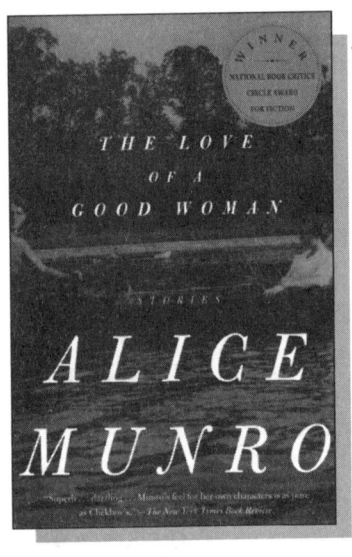

THE LOVE OF A GOOD WOMAN

Author: Alice Munro

Publisher: Vintage Books, 1999

Website: www.vintagebooks.com/read

Available in:
Paperback, 352 pages. $13.00
(ISBN 0-375-70363-2)

Genre: Fiction

Summary

In these eight stories, a master of the form extends and magnifies her great themes — the vagaries of love, the passion that leads down unexpected paths, the chaos hovering just under the surface of things, and the strange, often comical desires of the human heart. Time stretches out in some of the stories; in others it is telescoped. Some choices are made with irrevocable and surprising consequences. At other times disaster is courted or barely skirted. These beautifully told stories reveal life's rich layers and subtle implications, and in the process, expand the limits of fiction.

Recommended by: *The Washington Post Book World*

"Munro is indisputably a master ... A better book of stories can scarcely be imagined."

Author Biography

Alice Munro is the author of one novel and eight collections of short stories. She is a three-time winner of the Governor General's Literary Award, Canada's highest, and the W. H. Smith Award, given to her collection *Open Secrets* as the best book published in the United Kingdom in 1995. Her stories have appeared in *The New Yorker*, *The Paris Review*, and other publications, and her collections have been translated into thirteen languages.

Topics to Consider

1. In *The Love of a Good Woman*, how has the town of Jutland, its way of life and its mores, affected Enid's character and desires and helped to mold her into the person she is? What does she want from life and what compromises has she made?

2. What does the author accomplish by dividing *Jakarta* into two parts—the distant past and the present? In what essential way do the two marriages (Kath and Kent; Sonje and Cottar) differ? How are Kath's and Sonje's different attitudes to marriage borne out in the subsequent courses of their lives?

3. In *Cortes Island*, why did the narrator and her husband decide to marry, and how does the marriage evolve? Does the author imply that the same evolution occurs in most marriages?

4. In what ways are Eve and Sophie in *Save the Reaper* similar in character, and in what ways are they different? Would you say that Sophie, either consciously or unconsciously, has modeled her life on her mother's? If so, is the situation changing?

5. How does Pauline, in *The Children Stay*, perceive marriage and family life? Does the author imply that the pretenses and the feeling of imprisonment that Pauline experiences are present, to some degree, in every marriage? What role does the idea of fate play for the various characters?

6. How does Karin in *Rich As Stink* perceive the dynamic between Rosemary, Derek and Ann? How closely does her perception correspond with the reality? What sort of future do you envision for Rosemary? For Karin?

7. In *Before the Change*, how are the narrator's beliefs about abortion and parenthood affected by her own mother's death in childbirth, and how are these beliefs modified during the course of the story? How do her ideas about love undergo changes? Might she have made different decisions about her love affair and pregnancy if she had it to do over again?

8. In *My Mother's Dream*, what relation does Jill's struggle with the baby have to her struggle with George's family and his memory? Would you say that this mother-child struggle is a universal one, extreme though it is in Jill's case?

THE MANY LIVES AND SECRET SORROWS OF JOSEPHINE B.

Author: Sandra Gulland
Publisher: Scribner Paperback Fiction, 1999
Website: www.SimonSays.com
Available in: Paperback, 448 pages. $14.00 (ISBN 0-684-85606-9)
Genre: Historical Fiction

Summary

This is a dramatic tale of romance, heartbreak, and political intrigue set during the tumultuous times of the French Revolution. Combining meticulously researched history and superb storytelling, the author provides an intimate look into the lives of the men and women behind the revolution and relates Josephine Bonaparte's marvelous, perilous rise from an innocent girl to one of the most sophisticated and powerful women in history. Through her fictionalized diary entries, readers learn of the birth of her two children and the dissolution of her marriage due to her husband's indiscretions. She tells of her days of imprisonment during the bloody French Revolution and of the fall of the French monarchy. Finally, she writes of her husband's execution and of her fateful meeting with Napoleon Bonaparte with whom she will fulfill her destiny as Empress Josephine.

Recommended by: *Quill and Quire*
"A fascinating read from beginning to end."

Author Biography

Sandra Gulland was raised in the turmoil of the '60s in Berkeley, California. After emigrating to Canada in 1970, she taught school in a remote Inuit village before she began working in book publishing. She has been working on the Josephine novels for many years, traveling extensively to the places Josephine lived, learning to read French and corresponding with period scholars. She lives near Killlaloe, Ontario, with her husband and two children.

Topics to Consider

1. What are the benefits and/or drawbacks of telling a historical story in diary form? What techniques does the author use to make us believe in the authenticity of the diary?

2. How does destiny play a role in the lives of the different characters? What effect does knowing her fate ahead of time have on Josephine? What effect do the predictions have on you, the reader?

3. In her diary, Josephine often mentions the corset. How does the corset function as a metaphor for the role of women in this society before and after the revolution? What does it say about society as a whole?

4. What exactly is different after the revolution? Who is better off after the revolution and why? What has been gained, what has been lost?

5. What role did women play in Josephine's pre-Revolutionary France, and how did they change during the revolution? What did society value about women during this era?

6. How do Josephine's ideas about marriage change over the course of the story? Why does Josephine marry Bonaparte?

7. What kind of man is Alexandre? Is he a hypocrite or an honorable man? Is he arrogant or selfless? Give examples to back up your thinking. How do you reconcile Alexandre's heroic deeds in the revolution with his deceit in marriage? Can you think of any similar situations in today's world?

8. In what way does Josephine grow and change over the course of the story? In what ways does she stay the same?

9. Bonaparte tells Rose, "You think the woman I love does not exist. You don't believe in Josephine." Discuss how and why a name could have the power to change one's life.

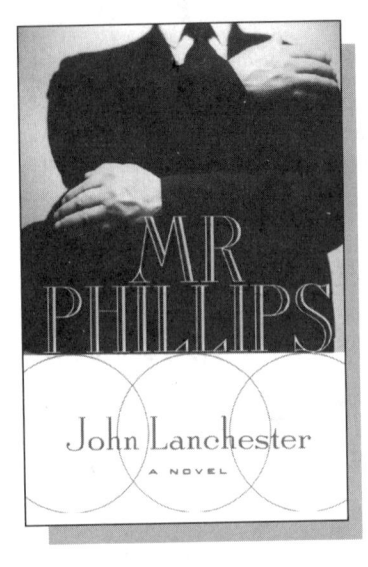

MR. PHILLIPS

Author: John Lanchester

Publisher: A Marian Wood Book/ Putnam, 1999

Website: www.penguinputnam.com

Available in: Hardcover, 304 pages. $23.95 (ISBN 0-399-14604-0)

Genre: Fiction

Summary

Mr. Phillips wakes on a Monday morning in his modest house, in the bed he has contentedly shared with his wife of nearly thirty years, ready to face another ordinary day. Except that this day is not ordinary, for on the previous Friday, Mr. Phillips was summarily sacked. Unable to deal with this disaster—unable even to tell his wife—Mr. Phillips rises at his usual hour and prepares himself, as he has done his entire working life, for the job he no longer has. Dressed for work with no work to do, Mr. Phillips wanders the streets of London, seeing the world as if for the first time. What he sees triggers memories, gradually building a portrait of a decent man who only 48 hours before knew exactly who and what he was—and on this day wonders who and what he can become.

Recommended by: Michael Upchurch, *Chicago Tribune*

"... A writer whose gifts border on the demonic."

Author Biography

John Lanchester's first novel, *The Debt to Pleasure*, was greeted with great critical acclaim. Translated into twenty-two languages, it won four major literary awards. Lanchester is the former Deputy Editor of the *London Review of Books*. Occasional pieces of his still appear there as well as in *The New Yorker* and *Granta*. He is now at work on his third novel, living in London.

Topics to Consider

1. What does the author accomplish by referring to his protagonist as "Mr. Phillips" as opposed to his first name? What is the significance of Lanchester's choice of Victor as Mr. Phillips' first name considering the events that befall the character?

2. How would you describe the depiction of women? What is your opinion of Mrs. Phillips and Clarissa Colingford? To what extent do you feel that this opinion is influenced by the fact that these women are described through the voice of Mr. Phillips instead of an impartial narrator?

3. In some sense, Mr. Phillips is a voyeur. In what sense is the reader also a voyeur in terms of observing both the people Mr. Phillips watches and Mr. Phillips himself?

4. Transitioning between chapters, Lanchester often makes an inexplicable jump in chronological order. How does this add to the mood of the novel? Is the author commenting on our tendency to "lose" parts of our day because of their monotony only to recall the specifics from memory if required to?

5. What do you make of Mr. Phillips' preoccupation with numbers and calculations? Does it contribute to his lack of emotional intensity or is it simply a manifestation of it?

6. What major comments do you feel this novel makes regarding the influence of the corporate world on our everyday lives?

7. In what ways does his experience with the bank robbery prove to be a maturation process for Mr. Phillips? Do you feel that his survival in the face of danger will provide enough of an impetus for him to tell Mrs. Phillips that he has been fired?

8. What compels Mr. Phillips to help the elderly woman with her grocery bags? Is this ultimately an act of kindness or an attempt by Mr. Phillips to reconfirm his own usefulness? In what ways does the story of Mr. Erith relate to that of Mr. Phillips?

9. How did you feel about the final line of the novel? Were you disappointed, or was it the appropriate way to finish the story? What do you see as the future of Mr. and Mrs. Phillips?

PEARS ON A WILLOW TREE

Author: Leslie Pietrzyk
Publisher: Bard/Avon Books, 1999
Website: www.avonbooks.com/bard
Available in:
Paperback, 280 pages. $12.50
(ISBN 0-380-79910-3)
Genre: Fiction

Summary

The Marchewka women are inseparable. They relish the joys of family gatherings, from preparing traditional holiday meals to organizing a wedding in which each of them is given a specific task. The foundation of a dignified, compassionate family, the women have learned to survive the hardships of emigration and assimilation in 20th century America. But as the century evolves, so does each succeeding generation. In this story, four generations of mothers and daughters of Polish ancestry are bound together by recipes, reminiscences and tangled relationships. It is a multigenerational roadmap of love and hate, distance and closeness, and the lure of the roots that both restrain and sustain us all.

Recommended by: *The Washington Post*

"... Gives us a sweating, crying, shouting, laughing group of women struggling to preserve and pass on that most precious of old family recipes: love."

Author Biography

Leslie Pietrzyk's fiction has been published in numerous literary journals, including *TriQuarterly, Iowa Review, Gettysburg Review,* and *New England Review.* She lives in Alexandria, Virginia, where she is at work on her second novel.

Topics to Consider

1. Why is this story not told chronologically? How does this reflect the motif of "time" that runs through the novel?

2. How would this book be different if it were told from only one point of view — for example, Amy's? Or Ginger's?

3. Why is Helen the only one of the four women who is never able to physically leave her mother?

4. How do each of the five superstitions in "Things Women Know" relate to the real lesson that follows?

5. Why does Amy decide to stay in Thailand for another year after meeting Taklaw? How does her decision compare to Ginger's decision to move to Phoenix? Rose's decision to leave Poland? Did they all leave for the same reasons?

6. How does Amy's sense of being foreign in Thailand compare with Rose's sense of being foreign in America? In what ways do Helen and Ginger feel "foreign"?

7. Does Ginger find redemption in the end? Does she ever understand herself? Is she understood by those around her?

8. Each woman struggles to find and maintain her own identity, separate from that of the family. Where and when does each woman feel most comfortable with herself?

9. Helen says, "A mother understands her daughter better than the daughter ever knows." (p. 257) Is this true for these mothers and daughters? Is it true for you?

10. "It's impossible for a good daughter to leave; it's impossible for a good daughter to stay," Rose says. Is the message of this novel that leaving one's family is bad? Is staying with one's family good?

11. "Pears on a willow tree with you — always wanting what's impossible," Rose says to Ginger. What "impossible pear" is each of these women looking for?

PEEL MY LOVE LIKE AN ONION

Author: Ana Castillo
Publisher: Doubleday, 1999
Website: www.randomhouse.com
Available in:
Hardcover, 224 pages. $23.95
(ISBN 0-385-49676-1)
Genre: Fiction

Summary

Carmen "La Coja" ("the cripple") Santos is a flamenco dancer of local renown in Chicago, despite the obstacle of a gimpy leg, the legacy of a childhood attack of polio. From the beginning of her professional career, she has carried on an affair with Agustin, the (married) director of her troupe — a romance that is going stale from overfamiliar lust and an absence of honesty. But when she begins a passionate liaison with the younger Manolo, Agustin's godson and a dancer of natural genius, an angry rivalry is sparked. Add to that the looming reassertion of her crippling disease and Carmen's vexed relations with her mother, and you have all the ingredients for a love story with equal parts soap opera, tragicomedy, and rhapsody.

Recommended by: Julia Alvarez, author of *Yo!*

"*Ana Castillo is* una *storyteller* de primera ... *able to hold our attention from the first to the last page of this packed, picaresque novel.*"

Author Biography

Ana Castillo is also the author of the novels *The Mixquiahuala Letters* and *Sapogonia*, the story collection *Loverboys*, the critical study *Massacre of the Dreamers*, and the poetry collection *My Father Was a Toltec*. She has won a Carl Sandburg Prize and an American Book Award. She lives in Chicago.

Topics to Consider

1. Ana Castillo quotes Simone De Beauvoir from *Memoirs of a Dutiful Daughter*, "My life would be a beautiful story come true, a story I would make up as I went along." How much of what we present to society is "a story we make up as we go along" and how much is true? How does Carmen reinvent herself as she goes along?

2. Given her disability, why do you think Carmen chooses her legs over her voice for the first part of her career? Have you ever chosen to follow a dream over what reality would seem to dictate? Is that what Carmen is doing?

3. Carmen spends two years in virtual isolation — as a potter in the desert. What comes out of this enforced solitude? What, if anything, does she learn about herself, her loves and her dreams?

4. Polio twice alters the course of Carmen's life. How do her childhood experiences, her schooling and her home life conspire to allow her to find a way out of the confines of her crippled body? Does her ability to transcend her circumstances seem improbable? What elements encourage or hinder her success?

5. Her relationships with Manolo and Agustin (the two major loves of her life) help her to feel whole but in reality prevent her from becoming successful, independent and content. Are the men responsible for this failure? What is Carmen's role? How does she finally escape this "confinement" to become her own person?

6. What attracts Carmen to the Calloro or gypsy culture as represented by her dancing and her connection to both Manolo and Agustin? By the end of the novel she seems to embody a merger of several cultures — the calloro (a free spiritedness), the gajes (a working stiff ethic) and the Spanish of her heritage. How do these cultures all work together to transform Carmen?

7. Ama discusses with her daughter the concept of Animo — that the soul and the body are inherently separate. Do you agree or disagree? Have you ever experienced the conflict that arises when the spirit desires to accomplish something that the physical limitations of one's body prevents? How did you reconcile this cross-purpose? How does Carmen?

A PLACE WITHOUT TWILIGHT

Author: Peter Feibleman
Publisher: LSU Press, 1997
Website: www.lsu.edu/guests/lsuprss
Available in:
Paperback, 382 pages. $14.95
(ISBN 0-8071-2225-4)
Genre: Fiction

Summary

In the New Orleans of the '30s and '40s, things—and people—are supposed to be black and white. Cille and her light-skinned brothers are neither. They are "the color that looks not-quite white next to a white man, and not-quite colored next to a colored man. It was a non-color in a place where you had to be something." The daughter of a dreamy alcoholic father who introduces Cille to "Mr. Keats and Mr. Shelley" but who exits her life too soon, and a mother who teaches her children not the love of God but the fear of him, young Cille struggles for balance and identity in a world where race and class define people for life, and where her brothers destroy themselves beating against the bars of the cage of a divided culture.

Recommended by: *New York Times*

"An artistic achievement ... An ardent new talent telling in fine, sensuous prose the story of an in-between Alice in a wonderland of blacks and whites."

Author Biography

Peter Feibleman, a native of New Orleans, is the author of numerous works – five novels, including *A Place Without Twilight* (first published in 1957); plays; screenplays; stories; books of nonfiction; and magazine articles. The recipient of a Guggenheim Fellowship and the Golden Pen Award, he lives in New York, on Martha's Vineyard, and in Barcelona with his wife, Susan.

Topics to Consider

1. Discuss the title as it relates to the main characters. Have you ever experienced "not fitting in?" How did you handle it? How do the Morris children handle it?

2. Discuss the role that music plays—from the structure of the book into movements to the mother's obsessive playing of *Thank God for a Garden*. What purpose does the music serve? How important is it to the central themes of the novel?

3. What are the similarities/differences between the female characters (both black and white)? How do they choose to live life in the face of alienation? What limitations, if any, does their skin color impose upon their choices?

4. Who or what is responsible for the difficult time the men in this novel seem to have? What role does Alva Morris play? Their multiracial displacement? How is Cille able to transcend this place of "not being" to find her place in the world? What place do the boys find for themselves?

5. For Lucille's mother, there is no in between—only black and white, right and wrong, good and bad. How does this affect her children? What tools do they employ to survive in this atmosphere? How has your parents' view of life influenced you?

6. The Morrises grow up in a house with two schools of thought—their mama's and their father's. What do the children learn from each of their parents?

7. The children hear the story of Florabelle and Dennis repeatedly. What is the significance of this story for them? What does it say about their father?

8. Many novels set in New Orleans cast the city itself as a major character. Did you feel that the setting was a crucial piece in telling this story? Could it have been set anywhere?

9. Cille feels that certain combinations (colors, for instance) beget certain outcomes (p. 293). Do you agree with this philosophy?

10. Some of life's largest questions are raised in this novel: Why do we live? Why do we die? How do Clarence, Dan and Cille answer these questions? How have you answered these questions in your own life?

PRETZEL LOGIC

Author: Lisa Rogak
Publisher: Williams Hill, 1999
Website: www.straightspouse.com
Available in:
Paperback, 256 pages, $15.00
(ISBN 0-9652502-4-5)
Genre: Fiction/Gender studies

Summary

What would you do if your spouse woke up and told you he was gay? Emily Spencer lived in Coventry, New Hampshire, with her husband Michael, where they published a weekly newspaper and were, by all accounts, happy. However, after a few years, Michael began to change; he grew quieter and more sullen. The more Emily pressed for an answer, the more he resisted. Finally, one day, she learned her husband's secret: Michael was gay. What follows is at turns bittersweet and hysterically funny as Emily and Michael learn to deal with their own truths. Recent movies like *In and Out* and *The Object of my Affection* have only skimmed the surface. *Pretzel Logic*, written by a woman who's been there, is the first story to tell it like it is.

Recommended by: Rebecca Rule, *The Concord (NH) Monitor*

"... reads like a blister bursting — full of anguish, anger, confusion, emotional turmoil. It reads true."

Author Biography

Lisa Rogak is the author of 25 nonfiction books. She lives in Grafton, New Hampshire, and was married to a man who came out during their marriage. *Pretzel Logic* has been featured in the *Washington Post* and the *Boston Globe*, and Rogak made her debut on The Oprah Winfrey Show in 1997.

Topics to Consider

1. If you didn't know a friend or co-worker was gay, how did you react after s/he came out?
2. Why did Emily think she and Michael could remain married after he came out? What do you think you would do?
3. Do you believe that sexual orientation is a characteristic that's fixed at birth, is defined by emotional trauma, or is a fluid trait destined to change throughout a person's life? How has this book changed your mind about sexual orientation?
4. Do you think that Michael would have stayed in the closet if he and Emily had stayed in the city? Did he postpone revealing his true sexual orientation because they moved to a small town?
5. The dynamics in *Pretzel Logic* closely resemble those in Grace Metalious' groundbreaking book *Peyton Place*. Discuss the similarities as well as the differences.
6. Emily compares her marriage to a rollercoaster after Michael comes out as gay. Both feel pulled between the reality and fantasy of a mixed-orientation marriage. How do you think a mixed-orientation marriage is similar to a heterosexual marriage where one of the partners has an affair? How do you think it's different?
7. Why do you think that Michael and Emily's marriage improved after Michael came out? Do you think this is the norm?
8. How do you think the experiences of straight men and straight women differ when their spouses come out?
9. Do you think that Emily was angrier at the fact that Michael was really gay or because he had been lying to her for all those years?
10. Do you believe that fewer gays and lesbians will feel compelled to hide in heterosexual marriages because of increased tolerance for homosexuality?

Editor's Note: The Pretzel Logic Online Book Club is the first book club of its kind. The conversation is ongoing, and members can join at will and jump in with comments or questions whenever the mood strikes instead of sticking to a set starting and ending date. See *www.onelist.com/community/Pretzel-Logic* for details.

THE RED TENT

Author: Anita Diamant
Publisher: Picador USA, 1998
Website: www.stmartins.com
Available in:
Paperback, 321 pages. $14.00
(ISBN 0-312-19551-6)
Genre: Fiction/Women's Studies

Summary

The Red Tent tells the little-known Biblical story of Dinah, daughter of the patriarch Jacob and his wife, Leah. In Chapter 34 of the Book of Genesis, Dinah's tale is a short, horrific detour in the familiar narrative of Jacob and Joseph. Anita Diamant imaginatively tells the story from the fresh perspective of its women. In the Biblical tale Dinah is given no voice, but she is the narrator of *The Red Tent*, which reveals the life of ancient womanhood — the world of the red tent.

Recommended by: James Carroll, author of *An American Requiem*

"The oldest story of all could never seem more original or more true."

Author Biography

Anita Diamant is a prize-winning jounalist whose work has appeared regularly in the *Boston Globe* and *Parenting* magazine. She is the author of five books about contemporary Jewish practice: *Choosing a Jewish Life, Bible Baby Names, The New Jewish Baby Book, The New Jewish Wedding,* and *Living a Jewish Life.* She lives in West Newton, Massachusetts, with her husband and daughter, Emilia, to whom *The Red Tent* is dedicated.

Topics to Consider

1. Does this book raise questions about other women in the Bible? Does it make you want to re-read the Bible and imagine other untold stories that lay hidden between the lines?

2. What do you make of the relationships among Jacob's four wives?

3. Dinah is rich in "mothers." Discuss the differences or similarities in her relationship with each woman.

4. How do the fertility, childbearing, and birthing practices differ from contemporary life? How do they compare with your own experience?

5. Discuss Jacob's role as a father. Does he treat Dinah differently from his sons? Does he feel differently about her? If so, how?

6. Female relationships figure largely in *The Red Tent*. Discuss the importance of Inna, Tabea, Werenro, and Meryt.

7. Dinah's point of view is often one of an outsider, an observer. What effect does this have on the narrative? What effect does this have on the reader?

8. The book travels from Haran (contemporary Iraq/Syria), through Canaan and Shechem (Israel), and into Egypt. What strikes you about the cultural differences Dinah encounters vis-à-vis food, clothing, work, and male-female relationships?

9. As Dinah grows from childhood to old age, discuss how she changes and matures. What lessons does she learn from life? If you had to pick a single word to describe the sum of her life, what word would you choose?

ROSIE'S PLACE
Offering Women Shelter and Hope

Author: Andrea Cleghorn

Publisher: VanderWyk & Burnham, 1997

Website: www.VandB.com

Available in:
Hardcover, 160 pages. $23.95
(ISBN 0-9641089-9-2)

Genre: Nonfiction/Social Issues/ Women's Studies

Summary

This nation's prototype drop-in shelter for women is more than a safe haven. Rosie's Place continues to set the example for giving the medical, legal, and educational assistance that allows women to walk back out the door with the one thing they most desperately need: a future. Experience the perspectives of guests and benefactors, staff and volunteers. One woman at a time, Rosie's Place offers support to each woman as she moves down the difficult and often frightening road to independence. Some of the women make it, and some of the women cannot.

Recommended by: Elizabeth Berg, author, *Durable Goods*

"This highly readable, even more highly inspirational book showed me how a woman's shelter can offer its residents so much more than food and lodging — namely, a sense of self-worth and a rebirth of hope. It also told me how volunteering at such a place very possibly does more for the volunteer than the client."

Author Biography

Andrea Cleghorn is a journalist, book reviewer, travel writer, and mother to two teenage children. Much of her research for this book took place in the dining room at Rosie's, where she worked the Friday lunch shift for two years.

Topics to Consider

1. Much like the author, the reader is an outside observer who is getting a glimpse into Rosie's Place. What do you find you "walked away" with, and what was it about this "experience" that makes you feel or think differently than you did before reading the book?

2. If you could have a discussion with one of the people in the book, which person would you like that to be, and why? What do you think you might learn from each other?

3. Rosie's Place is located in Boston, MA. If you live in or near a city, do you know whether it already has a sanctuary for women modeled on the Rosie's Place prototype? What aspect(s) of the prototype would you consider to be most critical to helping women help themselves?

4. The writing style of this book is sometimes reminiscent of a feature story in a newspaper, which is not surprising given that the author is a journalist. What effect does this style have on the story of Rosie's Place? If you were to write the story of Rosie's Place, what style of writing would you elect to use?

5. One of the themes that runs through the book is that volunteers at Rosie's Place seem to get as much out of their experience there as many of the clients get. Why do you think that is the case?

6. In what ways might you consider supporting the efforts of a sanctuary or shelter for women, from donating clothing or time or money to sponsoring internships at your place of business? What is your philosophy on helping the homeless? On preventing homelessness?

7. Consider the strength it takes for women to walk through the door at Rosie's Place — to ask for help. How do you think you would react if you found yourself abused or homeless, with no safe place to stay? How does that change your perspective on the problem of homelessness?

8. Fearless leader Kip Tiernan is not a young woman. What do you think "life after Kip" will be like at Rosie's Place?

SHE SAID YES
The Unlikely Martyrdom of Cassie Bernall

Author: Misty Bernall
Publisher: Plough Publishing House
Website: www.plough.com
Available in:
Hardcover, 160 pages. $17.00
(ISBN 0-87486-987-0)
Genre: Nonfiction/Family life

Summary

It's a fair bet that everyone has heard by now of the April, 1999 massacre at Columbine High School in Littleton, Colorado, and about Cassie Bernall, the student who was asked whether she believed in God and then was shot to death by two crazed classmates. It was her last word, but it echoed around the globe. Across the U.S. and throughout the world, newspapers and television channels hailed her as a "modern martyr." Her simple act of faith and bravery spoke to the deep recesses of people's hearts, and drew admiration from even the most cynical and jaded observers. But her parents knew only too well that behind the image of the stained-glass window saint portrayed by the media was a teenager who worried about her weight, her work, and her chances of finding a boyfriend. It's a story that her mother, Misty Bernall, tells with honesty and devotion. It's a story that everyone who cares about teens needs to read.

Recommended by: *Chicago Tribune*

"This is not a martyr's tale. It is a mourner's meditation—a mother's story of the death of a beloved and normal teenager."

Author Biography

In memory of their daughter—and in the hope that the violence that robbed her of her life might one day be turned into good—the Bernalls are devoting a portion of the proceeds from the sale of this book to a charitable foundation established in Cassie's name.

Topics to Consider

1. The book begins with the Columbine shooting. What fears did the Columbine tragedy raise for your child's safety (or for children you know) at school?

2. The book goes into depth about the troubled path Cassie was on. Why do you think that even in conscientious families kids sometimes go down the wrong path?

3. The Bernalls discovered Cassie's secret life by reading their daughter's private letters. Although this eventually led to positive results, did they have a right to "violate her privacy?" What "rights", if any, should parents respect?

4. What do you think was Mona's and Rick's influence on Cassie's deterioration? Do you think Cassie's parents were right in getting the sheriff to prevent them from seeing her?

5. Cassie's turnabout followed a weekend retreat. What role do you think it played in her life? What role do you think her parents' efforts played in Cassie making this dramatic change?

6. What lessons are there for parents in this story?

7. Both Cassie and her killers listened to music from artists like Marilyn Manson (p. 45). How do you feel about teens listening to this sort of music? How can parents and teens better connect when it comes to the issue of music?

8. Re-read Amanda's comments (page 60) that begin with "I went through a stage..." How important is it for teens to belong, to fit in? Do you remember wanting to find your place when you were in high school? Do you see your own children struggling to find their place?

9. Misty warns against viewing her daughter as a saint. Why?

10. Re-read the last paragraph on page 139. Can you see Cassie's death as not just a loss, but as a victory? How?

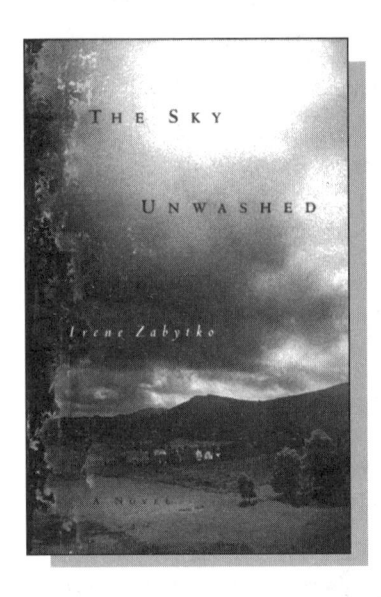

THE SKY UNWASHED

Author: Irene Zabytko

Publisher: Algonquin Books of Chapel Hill

Website: www.algonquin.com

Available in: Hardcover, 280 pages. $22.95 (ISBN 1-56512-246-1)

Genre: Fiction

Summary

This novel was inspired by the true story of the villagers who defied the forced evacuation of their Ukranian town after the nuclear accident at Chernobyl. One by one, the town's elders quietly returned to their homes. They did, they said, because they had nowhere else to go. *The Sky Unwashed* cuts through one of history's biggest political and environmental catastrophes to tell the story of one small village and people determined to live out their days in the place of their births.

Recommended by: W. D. Wetherell, author of *Chekhov's Sister*

"Zabytko's voice becomes the voice of the forgotten in a moving and memorable book."

Author Biography

A Ukranian American, Irene Zabytko grew up in Chicago. She now lives in Florida and has reviewed scores of books for the *Orlando Sentinel*. This is her first novel.

Topics to Consider

1. The Soviet media play an intriguing role in this story. Discuss the nature of the Soviet news, how it was interpreted, and how it was used by the people of Starylis to make decisions about their lives. Are there similarities to the American public's acceptance of "the news" from our own media?

2. Early in the story, Marusia has a dream and sees an image of the Virgin Mary "coming toward her with Her arms out, ready to catch something or someone." (Page 41) Discuss the meaning of this dream and how it relates to the ways life would unfold for Marusia.

3. Describe the changes to Marusia and Zosia's relationship from the beginning to the end of the story. What changes did you witness in Marusia? In Zosia? Were the changes valuable to either? In what ways?

4. The hardships of Soviet life presented several moral dilemmas throughout the book. Were the stealing, bribes, adultery and lies legitimate given the circumstances? Which acts could be considered necessary for survival? Which acts were inappropriate, regardless of the circumstances? Would your opinion differ if you answered the question from a Soviet, rather than an American, cultural perspective?

5. On his death bed, Yurko whispers to Zosia, "This time, I am leaving you." (Page 122) Discuss Yurko's feelings about his marriage as he spoke these words to his wife.

6. How is Marusia's decision to return to Starylis tested? Can you think of anyone in our society who feels as strongly about their sense of place?

7. Discuss the value of Marusia's ritual of ringing the bells.

8. Although Marusia's husband was unfaithful to her, she asks that Mychailyna be buried in the grave site next to Yurko's. Has she forgiven her husband? Has she forgiven Mychailyna? What can we learn about the act of forgiveness from her experience?

9. What is your opinion of the healer Lazorska's efforts and the intentions behind them?

10. If you were living in Starylis, what choices would you have made after the Chernobyl accident?

SOMETHING'S NOT RIGHT
One Family's Struggle with Learning Disabilities

Author: Nancy Lelewer
Publisher: VanderWyk & Burnham, 1994
Website: www.VandB.com
Available in: Paperback, 184 pages. $14.95 (ISBN 0-9641089-1-7)
Genre: Nonfiction/Family Issues/Parenting

Summary

"I stared at the page and total panic gripped me." The author's reaction to her reading test in first grade sets the stage for her book about learning disabilities in her family. Years later she would hear her son Brian ask, "Where is Wednesday, inside or out? I'll believe you when you show it to me." Daughter Kelly is quoted: "I go to school wearing a smile, but in my heart I'm dying." The author describes how she figured out, often on her own, the manner and content of instruction that would provide her children with an appropriate education.

Recommended by: *The Washington Post*

"An exciting, poignant story; a tale of how underachieving students and talented parents can overcome enormous obstacles."

Author Biography

Nancy Lelewer has been involved in dyslexia research at MIT and Harvard. Although her interests are varied, her real passions are her family and helping those with learning differences learn how to help themselves. She has developed games and a calendar specifically for helping young children understand space and time.

Topics to Consider

1. Think about what it took for the author to get the education each of her children needed. What actions might you have taken, either similar or different?

2. Why do you think the "experts" — at schools, at camps, in therapeutic settings — insist on communicating only with the child, avoiding or expressly forbidding conversation with the parents? What impact does this have on the author? How would you respond if you were in her place?

3. How has the book affected your understanding of the terms "emotionally disturbed" and "learning disabled"? Have the definitions and usage of these terms changed since the sixties, as far as you know? If yes, how and why have they changed?

4. Have you known someone with learning differences? If yes, how have the differences affected that person?

5. Studies have shown that a high percentage of prisoners have learning disabilities. Why do you think this may be true?

6. Teachers often have to balance the needs of special needs children against those of the rest of their classmates. Discuss the pros and cons of "mainstreaming" special needs children versus placing them in separate classes or schools. Consider the factors that administrators, teachers, and parents face in determining individual student placements.

7. What do you think about homeschooling? When might it be harmful to the child? When is it helpful?

STYGO

Author: Laura Hendrie
Publisher: MacMurray and Beck (2/00)
Website: www.macmurraybeck.com
Available in:
Paperback, 225 pages. $13.00
(ISBN 1-878448-94-3)
Genre: Fiction

Summary

Stygo, Colorado is the quintessential western town — a place where people work hard for very little and learn to survive on dreams. The author brings these dreamers to life in a haunting series of interlocked stories, including the tale of Tom, who suddenly finds his fantasy of moving to Alaska within reach; of Beca, struggling to free her older brother from the grip of their father's expectations; of Frank, who knows that love is a chimera often glimpsed but seldom captured; and of the other inhabitants, adults and children alike, who bear witness to love and despair and learn to take what they can from life.

Recommended by: E. Annie Proulx

"Stygo rocks with wild, hard writing."

Author Biography

Laura Hendrie lives in Ojo Sarco, New Mexico, where she helps manage a stone yard and stone fabricating shop. Her stories have been published in the *Missouri Review, Writer's Forum,* and the *Taos Review*. She has also contributed to several anthologies, including *Into the Silence, Best of the West I* and *III,* and *American Signatures*. She has won numerous awards for *Stygo*, including the 1995 American Academy of Arts and Letters Rosenthal Award, the 1995 Mountains & Plains Regional Book Award, and was a finalist for the 1995 PEN/Hemingway Foundation First Fiction Award.

Topics to Consider

1. How does the landscape form these lives? The weather?

2. What paths do individual characters take to escape? Is there more than one form of escape?

3. It's been said that this is a book about children. Why do you think this is? What role do they play?

4. What role does the amusement park play in the landscape of these lives?

5. Animals all seem to be aware on a level somewhere between that of adults and children. What use does the author make of animals and sentient ability?

SUGAR LAND

Author: Joni Rodgers
Publisher: Spinsters Ink, 1999
Website: www.spinsters-ink.com
Available in:
Paperback, 346 pages. $12.00
(ISBN 1-883523-32-X)
Genre: Fiction

Summary

This is the story of the Smithers sisters — Kit and Kiki. As children, they performed throughout Texas as the "Sugar Babes," but those glory days of county fair stages, adoring fans, and gold lamé gowns are long gone. Now Kit and Kiki are grown up. All that remains are the blues these sisters sing as they learn to cope with the vicissitudes of real life: withering marriages, cheating spouses, balloon mortgages, lost opportunities, the demands of motherhood. Then there's Neeva, Kit's mother-in-law-from-hell. And Mother Daubert, Kiki's perfectly-coiffed mother-in-law-from-denial-city. Both full of surprises.

Recommended by: *Southern Living*

"Every character in this novel resonates with life. This talented author knows how to bring paper-and-ink people to flesh-and-blood fulfillment."

Author Biography

Joni Rodgers was born into a family of bluegrass/gospel performers and grew up on stage, opening for Ernest Tubb, Grampa Jones, Patsy Montana, and other country legends. Her first novel, *Crazy for Trying* (MacMurray & Beck) was a finalist for the Barnes & Noble Discover Award. She lives with her husband, two children, and Redbone the dog in Houston, Texas.

Topics to Consider

1. How are Psyche and Eros used as a theme in this book? Why do you think the author uses this device?

2. Why was it important for Kiki to renew her singing career? What did she learn from it?

3. Mel refers to Kiki and Wayne's marriage as "a trailer house in a tornado" but he shies away from any involvement. Why?

4. Kit had sex with Ander. Her sister is going through a similar dilemma, from the other side of the fence. Why would Kit want to be the other woman?

5. What did the doves in Kiki's backyard represent?

6. Sugar Land is a place in Texas. But the title implies much more. What does Wayne say it refers to? What does it represent for Kiki and Kit?

7. Does sibling rivalry exist between Kiki and Kit? How does it affect their relationship?

8. There are several references to gold lamé throughout the story. What does it represent to Kit and Kiki?

9. Why did Kit go overboard with her paintings? What did this action represent to her?

10. When Mel explains to Kit about his mother's emotional involvement with Frank Dupuis, was it appropriate for Kit to express her secret, under the circumstances?

11. Even after the tornado, Kiki still loves Wayne. Why?

12. Kit was confused about the relationship of love and marriage. How does she resolve this dilemma? What did it mean to her to be a "good wife"?

13. The chapters of the book follow the stages of pregnancy. Why? What other theme is assumed?

SUMMER AT THE RESORT
Remembering the Fifties

Author: Henry Grady Starnes

Publisher: Starnes Publishing, 1997

Available in:
Paperback, 254 pages. $14.95
(ISBN 0-9657613-0-4)

Genre: Fiction/Memoir

Summary

History records the '50s as being a peaceful, tranquil, and fabulous era of our nation. The underlying theme of this book, though, is a contradiction of that impression. We fought a horrible war in Korea ... our basements were converted to bomb shelters in fear of a Russian atomic bomb attack ... we experienced the McCarthy hearings ... the Rosenbergs were executed on charges of treason. Racial tension flared with the integration of schools, and the nation was first exposed to Elvis Presley and rock and roll. As the young characters in this novel cycle between labor and lust in their resort world, they play out the despair, cynicism, and fear that gripped society at large.

Recommended by: Savannah Morning News

"... don't expect some rose-hued retrospective on the decade of 'Father Knows Best.' His characters definitely get into more than a bit of devilment."

Author Biography

Henry Grady Starnes grew up in the Atlanta, Georgia area during the Depression of the 1930s. He was able to attend college by working at a summer resort in New England. After serving in the Army he taught high school English and studied writing with Jesse Hill Ford. This is his first novel. *A Year of Deceit*, his newest book, will be published in June, 2000.

Topics to Consider

1. Does the story reflect the same impressions that you have of the '50s? If not, how do they differ?

2. Discuss the underlying themes of the story. How is despair, cynicism and fear played out by the characters?

3. How does the author capture the inexperience, frustration and awkwardness of these young characters? What do you think the behavior of present-day young men would be like under similar circumstances?

4. What is your reaction to Mario? Do you see him as opportunist and hard-nosed businessman who uses college students as cheap labor? Or is he a benevolent man who wants the students to have a good time and broaden their education?

5. Does the conflict between the waiters and the grounds crew have a substantial impact on the story? How does this conflict develop into a positive experience for the protagonist?

6. Of the four major romances in which Claxton is involved, which one do you think is more sincere, with the possibility of a lasting relationship? Which do you think is more important to him, the romance with Jean or the sexual encounter with Debbie?

7. How does the last chapter effectively bring the story to an end? What lines and actions of the characters show changes that have taken place in them?

8. How does the author use the prologue and the poem in developing the story?

9. Do you see any similarities between this story and J.D. Salinger's *Catcher in the Rye*?

SUNDAY YOU LEARN HOW TO BOX

Author: Bil Wright

Publisher: Scribner Paperback Fiction, (2/00)

Website: www.SimonSays.com

Available in: Paperback, 224 pages. $12.00 (ISBN 0-684-85795-2)

Genre: Fiction

Summary

Louis Bowman, the engaging young protagonist of this coming-of-age novel, is in the boxing ring both literally and metaphorically, fighting, as he says, "just to get to the end of the round." Riding out the emotional roller coaster of adolescence with his head and heart set spinning by the fist stirrings of sexual longing, Louis faces the violence in his home and the housing projects he hopes to one day escape. The author evokes Louis's world in vivid detail, from his stubborn, upwardly mobile mother, battling for her own life's dreams to be realized, to the enigmatic Ray Anthony Robinson, who give him the acceptance he longs for.

Recommended by: Karin Cook, author of *What Girls Learn*

"... Has all the rhythm, drama, and dance of a good fight ... In elegant and agile prose, Wright matches brutality with passion and heartbreak with hope."

Author Biography

Bil Wright is a fiction writer, poet, and playwright. Though this is his first novel, his fiction has appeared in several anthologies, including *Men on Men 3* and *Shades*. His poetry is anthologized in *The Road Before Us* and *The Name of Love*. He lives in New York City.

Topics to Consider

1. What is the relationship between love and danger in Louis's life? What does he risk by loving his mother? Ben? Ray Anthony?

2. After a fight between Louis and Ben, Louis's mother says to him, "Don't ruin what I'm trying to do here." What is she trying to do? How does her marriage to Ben figure into her goals? What does she expect from him? From Louis?

3. What is Jeanette's vision of a family? What is family supposed to achieve in her view? Do you agree or disagree with her view?

4. There is considerable pressure on Louis to "act like a man." What does that mean in his neighborhood and family?

5. Louis is fearful of the boys in the neighborhood, yet finds the courage to speak to Ray Anthony. What gives him the courage? Why does he feel drawn to Ray Anthony?

6. What is it about their personalities that keep Louis and his grandfather from communicating? How does their relationship with one another develop over time?

7. Why does Louis seek out Ed McMillan after the initial encounter on the train? Is he drawn to Ed as a father figure? A lover? A friend? Is he drawn to the danger?

8. Does your view of Jeanette change after she pierces Louis with a cooking fork? Is Jeanette now more of an enemy to Louis than Ben?

9. Can we accurately judge Jeanette's love for Louis by her actions toward him?

10. Based on what you know about Louis as a fourteen-year-old, what might the adult Louis Bowman be like?

11. What are some examples of Louis's forays into adulthood? How does he reach a sense of self in an environment that tries to quash it? What does he really want from life?

TALES OF PASSION, TALES OF WOE

Author: Sandra Gulland

Publisher: Scribner Paperback Fiction, 1999

Website: www.SimonSays.com

Available in:
Paperback, 384 pages. $14.00
(ISBN 0-684-85607-7)

Genre: Historical Fiction

Summary

The second installment of the Josephine trilogy begins on the day after her marriage to the "Corsican" Napoleon. We meet a mournful woman, beset by doubts, fearful of her children's reaction to her marriage and what the future may hold for all of them. Only two days after their marriage, Napoleon leaves Paris to take command of the Army of Italy. Josephine writes of her husband's triumphs and defeats, but it is the stresses of daily life that occupy her: the welfare of her children, aiding friends who plead for the benefit of her political contacts, the running of the household and the constant need for money to support the life that is appropriate to a woman of her station. This book recalls the extraordinary love story of the remarkable woman who captivated the man destined to change the world.

Recommended by: Nancy Wigston, *The Toronto Star*

"...*that rare phenomenon: a second novel even better than the first.*"

Author Biography

Sandra Gulland was raised in the turmoil of the '60s in Berkeley, California. After emigrating to Canada in 1970, she taught school in a remote Inuit village before she began working in book publishing. She has been working on the Josephine novels for many years, traveling extensively to the places Josephine lived, learning to read French and corresponding with period scholars. She lives near Killlaloe, Ontario, with her husband and two children.

Topics to Consider

1. What were some of the most pressing issues of the time? What is the most interesting aspect of this period of French history?

2. Josephine speaks of her love for Napoleon but also admits in her diary that he is, in many ways, a stranger to her. What may have been her reasons for the marriage? How did her feelings for him change over time?

3. Josephine initially kept the fact of her marriage to Napoleon hidden from her two young children. From a modern perspective, how might Josephine have eased the situation for both her children and her new husband?

4. Napoleon's family appears to be a venal lot at best — all of them plotted continually against outsiders and even each other. Many modern marriages are similarly assaulted by family members with varying agendas. What differences do you perceive between the late eighteenth century and modern times in this regard?

5. Discuss the pressures that beset their marriage from the outset. Given their respective characters, what might a meeting between the couple and a modern marriage counselor have been like?

6. Were Josephine's financial involvements ethically questionable? Would her financial situation and dealings be viewed differently if she had been a man?

7. How do Napoleon and Josephine seem as people? More or less as history has depicted them? Which characteristics do you admire? Which do you deplore?

8. Josephine fulfilled many traditional roles: mother, wife, hostess. She also involved herself in politics and business. Did she wield power? If so, in what way, and to what end? What role did she play in Napoleon's rise to power? Of all her roles, which do you think was the most important to her?

UNFORGOTTEN

Author: D. J. Meador
Publisher: Pelican Publishing, 1999
Website: www.pelicanpub.com

Available in:
Hardcover, 400 pages. $25.00
(ISBN 1-56554-349-1)

Genre: Fiction

Summary

In 1951 a hardened young Army lieutenant, John Winston, must balance his belief in the United Nations' mission with his contempt for the seemingly futile methods used to achieve it. More than forty years later, Winston is a successful Alabama trial lawyer who has put his military service behind him. John is surprised to learn that he is being considered for a federal judgeship. Phone calls pour in from people offering support and encouragement. One call, however, is different. "Were you in Korea in 1951?" asks a strange female voice. "I know what happened there—know what you did. If you get nominated, I'll tell." John's senses go on full alert. He had told no one, not even his late wife, about what had gone on. Yet someone knew—and was willing to destroy his future by exposing his past.

Recommended by: *Publishers Weekly*

"... Contributes notably to the exploration of the issues surrounding America's so-called forgotten war."

Author Biography

D.J. Meador is Professor Emeritus at the University of Virginia School of Law. In *Unforgotten,* he draws on his tour of duty during the Korean War, where he served as an officer in the U.S. Army's Judge Advocate General's Corps. Meador's first novel, *His Father's House* (Pelican, 1994), has been optioned for a motion picture.

Topics to Consider

1. John Winston grows up in the post-war south, where a code of honor and hero worship is ingrained. Who are John's heroes at the start? Have they changed by the close of the novel? Does he still have heroes? In what ways is this a particularly Southern story? In what ways is this an American Story?

2. The differences between the three women in Winston's life, Jeanie, Sally and Henny, are profound. Explain how each woman symbolizes the condition of his life at the time that they are important to him.

3. The role of theology in war has great significance for Winston. How does he view God's role in wartime? How do his views change as he struggles to understand all that he has experienced? Ultimately, he seems to feel that God doesn't promise us an easy life, He merely promises to be with us. Do you agree or disagree with this view of God's role?

4. At one point in his Korean experience, Winston's fear evaporates as a "kill or be killed" mentality takes over. What causes this change and how does it influence his actions? Have you ever experienced anything like this shift in feeling and perspective?

5. What does war teach John Winston? How does his experience in Korea alter his opinion of other wars and the high-profile people involved in them? On a personal level, how does it affect his attitudes about his grandfather's participation in the Civil War and his father's in World War I?

6. Winston has a life prior to his involvement in Korea and a life after, but has difficulty connecting the two. How does he finally build a bridge between the person he was and the person he has become? By the end of the story, has he merged his two lives successfully?

7. In the course of his court-martial, Winston is faced with the concept of justice under law versus the concept of pure justice or justice under God. What are the differences and similarities between these concepts? How does he reconcile the conflicts posed by these two forms of justice? How do you?

WHERE RIVER TURNS TO SKY

Author: Gregg Kleiner

Publisher: Bard Books (Avon), 1999

Website: www.AvonBooks.com/Bard

Available in:
Paperback, 379 pages. $12.50
(ISBN 0-380-80559-6)

Genre: Fiction

Summary

Eighty-year-old George Castor promised he would never let his best friend Ralph die alone at the Silver Gardens Nursing Home — but Ralph passed on while George was away fishing. Distraught, guilt-stricken, and seeking redemption, George buys a broken-down mansion in Oregon, paints it fire-engine red, and begins searching for other old folks to share it with him. Because George has made a new promise that will alter the course of the rest of his life. And, with the help of a miraculous old woman named Grace, he assembles a ragtag bunch of aging strangers, determined to make their last days on earth — and his own — an adventure.

Recommended by: Terry Kay, author

"An absolute triumph of storytelling ... [Kleiner] dignifies aging and the human experience in one of the most wonderfully written novels of our time."

Author Biography

Gregg Kleiner has worked as a dairy goat farmer, hotel concierge, freelance journalist, wildlife biologist, and technical writer. He now lives in western Oregon with his wife, Lori, and their two small children. *Where River Turns to Sky* is his first novel.

Topics to Consider

1. What is the purpose of the free-floating passages found throughout the book, for example, "Moon on Wet Concrete"? Do they clarify or confuse things for the reader?

2. Did you want more information about why things "went wrong" with George's son, Jason, or was his death merely the means to an end in the story?

3. What drives George Castor? Is it simply his desire to do right by Ralph, or is it something more?

4. Nature is a unifying theme in the book. Give examples of how the natural world affects George, Clara, and Grace.

5. How does the author tie in imagery throughout the book, for example, the star?

6. One might describe Clara as a "quiet observer." What roles do the other characters assume?

7. Did you take Grace's death speech (page 328) as a predictor of her own mortality, or nothing more than moving words for George's ears? Did her suicide shock you?

8. Were you surprised when "Amy" appeared out of nowhere?

9. Some might consider the ending trite, with the return of Mr. Liu, Amy and her daughter coming to help, and Mrs. Beasley agreeing to move in. How did you feel about the ending? Were you disappointed, or did you want things to end up neatly, so to speak?

10. What age do you think the author to be? Were his descriptions and perspectives of old age accurate and believable?

ZABELLE

Author: Nancy Kricorian
Publisher: Bard/Avon Books, 1999
Website: wwwavonbooks.com/bard
Available in:
Paperback, 240 pages. $12.50
(ISBN 0-380-73211-4)
Genre: Fiction

Summary

As Zabelle's family assembles for her funeral in present-day Massachusetts, it becomes clear that her children hardly knew her. But as this alternately comic and heartbreaking novel unfolds—beginning with Zabelle's survival of the 1915 Armenian Genocide in Turkey and her subsequent emigration to America for an arranged marriage—an unforgettable character emerges.

Recommended by: The New Yorker

"Affecting ... haunting and convincing ... there's a fairy tale quality to the prose — a sense of wondrous and terrible things happening apart from human volition."

Author Biography

Nancy Kricorian was raised in Watertown, Massachusetts, which has had a large Armenian community since the 1920s. With degrees from Dartmouth College and Columbia University, Kricorian is a widely published and award-winning poet who currently lives in New York City with her husband and their two daughters.

Topics to Consider

1. Discuss those instances in the story when quick judgments influenced Zabelle's behavior. How were her children influenced as a result?

2. The book refers to an Armenian custom (page 63) called "the bride has lost her tongue." How did this custom apply to Zabelle's marriage with Toros? Discuss how her approach to communicating with her husband changed as the story unfolds.

3. It is decided that Zabelle would not continue her English class. Discuss how this decision was made and what it says about Toros' character. Zabelle says, "Now I knew that I was on my own." Discuss what she does differently after this event to claim a life of her own.

4. Discuss Zabelle's relationship with Vartanoush, her mother-in-law. How does it influence the way she later relates to her sons' wives?

5. For decades, Zabelle, her friend Arsinee, and Toros chose not to talk about the horrors they witnessed early in their lives. What were the drawbacks to their silence? Was Zabelle's silence the cause of her dreams? Were there benefits to the silence?

6. How would the marriage of Zabelle and Toros been different had they openly spoken about their stories of hardship earlier in the relationship?

7. When Moses, Zabelle's son, tells her that God had spoken to him — to change his name and his nose — Zabelle claims he's gone crazy. (Page 156) Arsinee suggests that "his nose will come back to haunt him on the face of his children." (Page 161) How do Zabelle and Toros handle the choices their sons make? Does Zabelle react differently when Joy considers marriage?

8. Discuss Arsinee's role in the telling of this story. What does she offer Zabelle? What does her character offer the reader?

9. Could Zabelle's children have known her any better than they did at her funeral?

10. In what ways are the choices and perspectives of younger generations in the Chahasbanian family similar to those of children from other immigrant families? How are they different?

Books to Talk About
at Your Next Reading Group

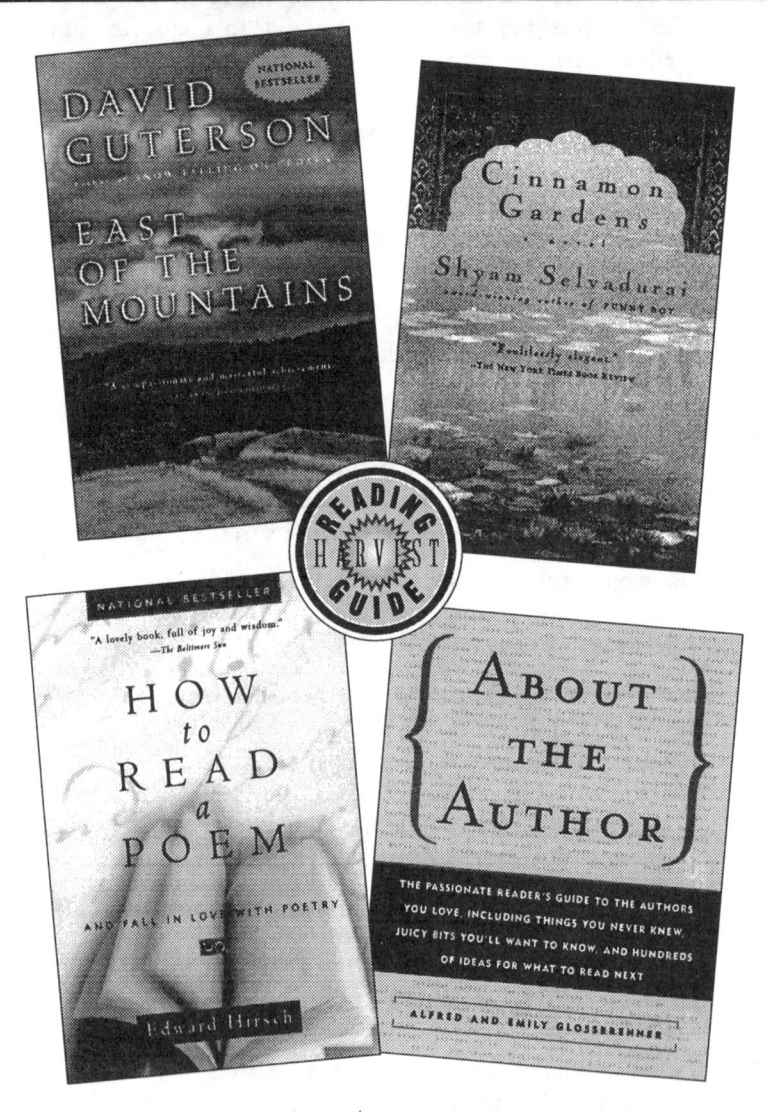

Harcourt | HARVEST BOOKS

SPECIAL OFFER

Add something new and exciting to your next meeting by including the author in your discussion

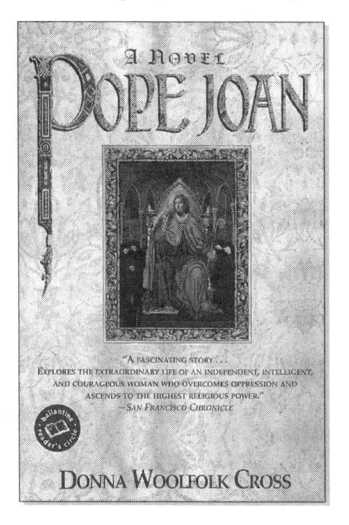

She is the legend that will not die — Pope Joan, the first and only woman ever to sit on the throne of St. Peter. This stirring novel, based on historical record, brings the Dark Ages to life in all their brutal splendor and shares the dramatic story of an unforgettable woman, reminiscent of Jane Austen's Emma, Jean Auel's Ayla, and other heroines who struggle against restrictions their souls will not accept.

Donna Woolfolk Cross, author of the international bestseller *Pope Joan*, will chat by speakerphone with book discussion groups. This special offer has been made in conjunction with the launch of Ballantine's new Reader's Circle Books, designed specifically for reading groups. Every copy of *Pope Joan* has discussion questions, an interview with the author, and provocative reviews bound right into the back of the book itself.

Interested reading groups can leave a message on the guestbook of the *Pope Joan* website (*www.popejoan.com*) or they can fax the author directly at 315-469-1680. The author will contact them to set up a mutually convenient time for a chat.

Pope Joan
Ballantine Books, 1997
Paperback, 422 pages, $12.95
ISBN 0-345-41626-0

Visit the most comprehensive reading group resource **anywhere on the Web**.... Newly **expanded** and **redesigned**.

VINTAGE BOOKS
READING GROUP CENTER
THE READING GROUP SOURCE FOR BOOKLOVERS

Features:

Tips	• Get **ideas** for your meeting or **information** on how to join a reading group	**PLUS:**
Planner	• Plan ahead with a **sneak peek** at future reading group selections from Vintage	**What's New:** An at-a-glance guide to new features on the site
Cheat Sheet	• Prepare for your discussion with **author interviews, excerpts, reviews**, and more	**Best Books List:** The best books for discussion— from reading group members across the country.
Reading Group Guides	• View a complete list of **over 80 Vintage Reading Group Guides** by title or category	
Recommendations	• Read our **newsletters** online and sign up to receive **recommendations by e-mail**	
Reader's Board	• **Interact** with other readers on our bulletin board	**On the Road:** A list of upcoming author events
Vintage Home	• Find more **great books in paperback** from Vintage	**Novel Ideas:** Words of advice from other readers

www.vintagebooks.com/read

RESOURCES

The Internet

Reading Group Choices Online — Includes a directory of over 550 guides available from publishers as well as more than 200 guides that can be printed directly from the site.
www.readinggroupchoices.com

Publisher Web Sites — Find additional topics for discussion, special offers for book groups, and other titles of interest.

Algonquin Books of Chapel Hill — *www.algonquin.com*
Avon Books — *www.avonbooks.com*
Curbstone Press — *www.curbstone.org*
Harcourt Brace — *www.harcourt.com*
HarperCollins — *www.harpercollins.com*
Henry Holt & Co. — *www.henryholt.com*
Louisiana State University Press — *www.lsu.edu/guests/lsuprss*
MacMurray and Beck — *www.macmurraybeck.com*
Milkweed Editions — *www.milkweed.org*
Pelican Publishing — *www.pelicanpub.com*
Plough Publishing — *www.plough.com*
Penguin Putnam — *www.penguinputnam.com/guides/index.htm*
Picador / St. Martin's Press — *www.stmartins.com/rgg.htm*
RH / Bantam Doubleday Dell — *www.randomhouse.com*
Scribner / Simon & Schuster — *www.simonsays.com*
Spinsters Ink — *www.spinsters-ink.com*
University of Missouri Press — *www.system.missouri.edu/upress*
University Press of Kentucky — *www.uky.edu/UniversityPress*
VanderWyk & Burnham — *www.VandB.com*
Vintage Books / Random House — *www.vintagebooks.com/read*
W.H. Freeman — *www.whfreeman.com*
William Morrow & Co. — *www.williammorrow.com*
Williams Hill Publishing — *www.straightspouse.com*

Newsletters

Book Club Today, an upbeat, innovative bimonthly publication for book club members and leaders. The most comprehensive guide for book club news. Issues contain book club profiles, national book club trends, reading group events and literary travel, themes for meetings, book reviews, and discussion questions. A great gift for the reading enthusiast! Annual subscription is $24.95 US (6 issues). Send postal mailing address to:
BookClubToday@aol.com or
Book Club Today
PO Box 210165
Cleveland, OH 44121-7165
www.BookClubToday.com

Book Lovers, quarterly book review publication with recommendations by the editor and librarians. Subscription: $10/yr. Contact:
Book Lovers
PO Box 511396
Milwaukee, WI 53203-0241
(414)384-2300
www.execpc.com/~booklove

Booknews and Views, quarterly newsletter of Books, Etcetera. Annual subscription is $10. Contact:
Books, Etcetera
228 Commercial Street #1957
Nevada City, CA 95959
(530) 478-9400

Reverberations News Journal, Rachel Jacobsohn's publication of the Association of Book Group Readers and Leaders. Annual membership including subscription is $18. Contact:
ABGRL
Box 885
Highland Park, IL 60035
(847) 266-0431
E-mail: *rachelj@interaccess.com*

Literary Travel

FPT Special Interest Tours. Annual trips with Diana Altman, Women's National Book Association member and travel consultant. Contact:

FPT
186 Alewife Brook Parkway
Cambridge, MA 02138
phone (800) 645-0001, fax (617) 661-3354
E-mail: *dma@fpt.com*

Literary Getaways with Judith Palarz. Book discussions and sightseeing for lovers of literature. Two days, two nights at a Bed & Breakfast Inn in Nevada City, the Napa Valley, Half Moon Bay, and other locations. Contact:

Books, Etcetera
228 Commercial Street #1957
Nevada City, CA 95959
(530) 478-940

Books & Journals

The Book Group Book: A Thoughtful Guide to Forming and Enjoying a Stimulating Book Discussion Group. Edited by Ellen Slezak and Margaret Eleanor Atwood. Published by Chicago Review Press, ISBN 1-5565-2246-0, $12.

Circles of Sisterhood: A Book Discussion Group Guide for Women of Color by Pat Neblett. Published by Writers & Readers, ISBN 0-8631-6245-2, $14.

Family Book Sharing Groups: Start One in Your Neighborhood! by Marjorie R. Simic and Eleanor C. MacFarlane. Published by Grayson Bernard Publishers, ISBN 1-8837-9011-5, $6.95.

The Go On Girl! Book Club Guide for Reading Groups: Works Worth Reading, Chats with Our Favorite Authors, by Monique Greenwood, Lynda Johnson and Tracy Mitchell-Brown. Published by Little, Brown & Co., ISBN 0-7868-8350-2, $14.95

Minnesota Women's Press Great Books.
Contact: Minnesota Women's Press, 771 Raymond Avenue, Saint Paul, MN 55114, (612) 646-3968.

Books & Journals (continued)

The Mother-Daughter Book Club: How Ten Busy Mothers and Daughters Came Together to Talk, Laugh and Learn Through Their Love of Reading by Shireen Dodson and Teresa Barker. Published by HarperCollins, ISBN 0-0609-5242-3, $14.00.

The Reading Group Handbook: Everything You Need to Know to Start Your Own Book Club by Rachel W. Jacobsohn. Published by Hyperion, ISBN 0-7868-8324-3, $11.95.

Reading Group Journal: Notes in the Margin. Published by Abbeville Press, ISBN 0-7892-0586-6, $16.95.

The Reading List: Contemporary Fiction, A Critical Guide to the Complete Works of 110 Authors. Edited by David Rubel. Published by Owl Books, ISBN 0-805055-27-4, $15.95.

Reading to Heal: A Reading Group Strategy for Better Health by Diane Dawber. Published by Quarry Press, ISBN 1-5508-2229-2, $6.95.

Talking About Books: A Step-by-Step Guide for Participating in a Book Discussion Group by Marcia Fineman. Published by Talking About Books, ISBN 0-9661-5670-6, $11.95.

What to Read: The Essential Guide for Reading Group Members and Other Book Lovers by Mickey Pearlman. Published by HarperCollins, ISBN 0-0609-5313-6, $14.00.

BOOK GROUP MEMBERS

Name _____
    Day phone _____ Eve. phone _____

Name _____
    Day phone _____ Eve. phone _____

Name _____
    Day phone _____ Eve. phone _____

Name _____
    Day phone _____ Eve. phone _____

Name _____
    Day phone _____ Eve. phone _____

Name _____
    Day phone _____ Eve. phone _____

Name _____
    Day phone _____ Eve. phone _____

Name _____
    Day phone _____ Eve. phone _____

Name _____
    Day phone _____ Eve. phone _____

Name _____
    Day phone _____ Eve. phone _____

Name _____
    Day phone _____ Eve. phone _____

BOOK GROUP MEETING DATES

January _____

February _____

March _____

April _____

May _____

June _____

July _____

August _____

September _____

October _____

November _____

December _____

January _____

February _____

March _____

2000

January
S	M	T	W	T	F	S
						1
2	3	4	5	6	7	8
9	10	11	12	13	14	15
16	17	18	19	20	21	22
23/30	24/31	25	26	27	28	29

February
S	M	T	W	T	F	S
		1	2	3	4	5
6	7	8	9	10	11	12
13	14	15	16	17	18	19
20	21	22	23	24	25	26
27	28	29				

March
S	M	T	W	T	F	S
			1	2	3	4
5	6	7	8	9	10	11
12	13	14	15	16	17	18
19	20	21	22	23	24	25
26	27	28	29	30	31	

April
S	M	T	W	T	F	S
						1
2	3	4	5	6	7	8
9	10	11	12	13	14	15
16	17	18	19	20	21	22
23/30	24	25	26	27	28	29

May
S	M	T	W	T	F	S
	1	2	3	4	5	6
7	8	9	10	11	12	13
14	15	16	17	18	19	20
21	22	23	24	25	26	27
28	29	30	31			

June
S	M	T	W	T	F	S
				1	2	3
4	5	6	7	8	9	10
11	12	13	14	15	16	17
18	19	20	21	22	23	24
25	26	27	28	29	30	

July
S	M	T	W	T	F	S
						1
2	3	4	5	6	7	8
9	10	11	12	13	14	15
16	17	18	19	20	21	22
23/30	24/31	25	26	27	28	29

August
S	M	T	W	T	F	S
		1	2	3	4	5
6	7	8	9	10	11	12
13	14	15	16	17	18	19
20	21	22	23	24	25	26
27	28	29	30	31		

September
S	M	T	W	T	F	S
					1	2
3	4	5	6	7	8	9
10	11	12	13	14	15	16
17	18	19	20	21	22	23
24	25	26	27	28	29	30

October
S	M	T	W	T	F	S
1	2	3	4	5	6	7
8	9	10	11	12	13	14
15	16	17	18	19	20	21
22	23	24	25	26	27	28
29	30	31				

November
S	M	T	W	T	F	S
			1	2	3	4
5	6	7	8	9	10	11
12	13	14	15	16	17	18
19	20	21	22	23	24	25
26	27	28	29	30		

December
S	M	T	W	T	F	S
					1	2
3	4	5	6	7	8	9
10	11	12	13	14	15	16
17	18	19	20	21	22	23
24/31	25	26	27	28	29	30

2001

January
S	M	T	W	T	F	S
	1	2	3	4	5	6
7	8	9	10	11	12	13
14	15	16	17	18	19	20
21	22	23	24	25	26	27
28	29	30	31			

February
S	M	T	W	T	F	S
				1	2	3
4	5	6	7	8	9	10
11	12	13	14	15	16	17
18	19	20	21	22	23	24
25	26	27	28			

March
S	M	T	W	T	F	S
				1	2	3
4	5	6	7	8	9	10
11	12	13	14	15	16	17
18	19	20	21	22	23	24
25	26	27	28	29	30	31

April
S	M	T	W	T	F	S
1	2	3	4	5	6	7
8	9	10	11	12	13	14
15	16	17	18	19	20	21
22	23	24	25	26	27	28
29	30					

May
S	M	T	W	T	F	S
		1	2	3	4	5
6	7	8	9	10	11	12
13	14	15	16	17	18	19
20	21	22	23	24	25	26
27	28	29	30	31		

June
S	M	T	W	T	F	S
					1	2
3	4	5	6	7	8	9
10	11	12	13	14	15	16
17	18	19	20	21	22	23
24	25	26	27	28	29	30

July
S	M	T	W	T	F	S
1	2	3	4	5	6	7
8	9	10	11	12	13	14
15	16	17	18	19	20	21
22	23	24	25	26	27	28
29	30	31				

August
S	M	T	W	T	F	S
			1	2	3	4
5	6	7	8	9	10	11
12	13	14	15	16	17	18
19	20	21	22	23	24	25
26	27	28	29	30	31	

September
S	M	T	W	T	F	S
						1
2	3	4	5	6	7	8
9	10	11	12	13	14	15
16	17	18	19	20	21	22
23/30	24	25	26	27	28	29

October
S	M	T	W	T	F	S
	1	2	3	4	5	6
7	8	9	10	11	12	13
14	15	16	17	18	19	20
21	22	23	24	25	26	27
28	29	30	31			

November
S	M	T	W	T	F	S
				1	2	3
4	5	6	7	8	9	10
11	12	13	14	15	16	17
18	19	20	21	22	23	24
25	26	27	28	29	30	

December
S	M	T	W	T	F	S
						1
2	3	4	5	6	7	8
9	10	11	12	13	14	15
16	17	18	19	20	21	22
23/30	24/31	25	26	27	28	29

INDEX BY SUBJECT/INTEREST AREA

Addiction/Recovery 26
Adventure 20, 36
African-American 70, 90
Aging 96
Appalachian Studies 24
Asian-American 34
Biography 54, 62, 92
Coming of Age 14, 50, 90
Contemporary Life 46
Education 82
Family Issues 18, 38, 66, 78, 82, 98
Gay/Lesbian 26, 72
Gender Studies 72
Government/Politics 36
History 62, 92
Inspiration 56
Jewish Studies 74
Love 42, 68
Meaning of Life 28, 32, 60, 64,
Memoir 12, 16, 24, 34, 88
Morals/Ethics 28, 52
Mother-Daughter Relationships 14, 38, 66, 78
Multicultural Studies 40, 70
Native American 40
Parenting 82
Personal Triumph 12, 16, 20, 24, 26, 34, 54,
Relationships 18, 46, 86
Religion 36
Roman à Clef 30

INDEX BY SUBJECT/INTEREST AREA

(continued)

Small-town life   14, 44, 54, 80, 84
Social/Cultural Issues   56, 76, 88
Spirituality   56
Therapy   52
War, effects of   22, 48, 88, 94, 98
Women's Studies   24, 52, 54, 74, 76,
World Studies   16, 22, 34, 48, 58, 62, 80, 92
Writing   50

INDEX BY AUTHOR

Andrews, Gregg   page 54
INSANE SISTERS

Bernall, Misty   page 78
SHE SAID YES

Castillo, Ana   page 68
PEEL MY LOVE LIKE AN ONION

Cleghorn, Andrea   page 76
ROSIE'S PLACE

Cunningham, Michael   page 46
THE HOURS

DeRosier, Linda Scott   page 24
CREEKER: A WOMAN'S JOURNEY

Diamant, Anita   page 74
THE RED TENT

Feibleman, Peter   page 70
A PLACE WITHOUT TWILIGHT

Gulland, Sandra   page 62
THE MANY LIVES & SECRET SORROWS OF JOSEPHINE B.

Gulland, Sandra   page 92
TALES OF PASSION, TALES OF WOE

Guterson, David   page 28
EAST OF THE MOUNTAINS

Hendrie, Laura   page 84
STYGO

Henley, Patricia   page 48
HUMMINGBIRD HOUSE

Kleiner, Gregg   page 96
WHERE RIVER TURNS TO SKY

Kricorian, Nancy   page 98
ZABELLE

Lanchester, John   page 64
MR. PHILLIPS

INDEX BY AUTHOR
(continued)

Lelewer, Nancy *SOMETHING'S NOT RIGHT*	page 82
Lott, Deborah A. *IN SESSION*	page 52
McKracken, Elizabeth *THE GIANT'S HOUSE*	page 42
McNeal, Tom *GOODNIGHT, NEBRASKA*	page 44
Meador, D. J. *UNFORGOTTEN*	page 94
Michener, Marian *DREAMING UNDER A TON OF LIZARDS*	page 26
Minot, Susan *EVENING*	page 32
Munro, Alice *THE LOVE OF A GOOD WOMAN*	page 60
Nicol, Margaret *ENEMY OF THE AVERAGE*	page 30
O'Faolain, Nuala *ARE YOU SOMEBODY?*	page 16
Pietrzyk, Leslie *PEARS ON A WILLOW TREE*	page 66
Rodgers, Joni *SUGAR LAND*	page 86
Rogak, Lisa *PRETZEL LOGIC*	page 72
Santiago, Esmeralda *ALMOST A WOMAN*	page 12
Saracino, Mary *FINDING GRACE*	page 38
Schulman, Audrey *THE CAGE*	page 20

INDEX BY AUTHOR
(continued)

Sidhwa, Bapsi — *CRACKING INDIA* — page 22

Silko, Leslie Marmon — *GARDENS IN THE DUNES* — page 40

Smith, Dodie — *I CAPTURE THE CASTLE* — page 50

Starnes, Henry Grady — *SUMMER AT THE RESORT* — page 88

Strout, Elizabeth — *AMY AND ISABELLE* — page 14

Thomas, William H. — *LEARNING FROM HANNAH* — page 56

Walton, Lewis R. — *FINAL STORM* — page 36

Wright, Bil — *SUNDAY YOU LEARN HOW TO BOX* — page 90

Yamanaka, Lois-Ann — *BLU'S HANGING* — page 18

Yen Mah, Adeline — *FALLING LEAVES* — page 34

Zabytko, Irene — *THE SKY UNWASHED* — page 80

INDEX BY GENRE

Nonfiction

ALMOST A WOMAN	page	12
ARE YOU SOMEBODY?	page	16
CREEKER: A WOMAN'S JOURNEY	page	24
FALLING LEAVES	page	34
IN SESSION	page	52
INSANE SISTERS	page	54
ROSIE'S PLACE	page	76
SHE SAID YES	page	78
SOMETHING'S NOT RIGHT	page	82

Fiction

AMY AND ISABELLE	page	14
BLU'S HANGING	page	18
THE CAGE	page	20
CRACKING INDIA	page	22
DREAMING UNDER A TON OF LIZARDS	page	26
EAST OF THE MOUNTAINS	page	28
ENEMY OF THE AVERAGE	page	30
EVENING	page	32
FINAL STORM	page	36
FINDING GRACE	page	38
GARDENS IN THE DUNES	page	40
THE GIANT'S HOUSE	page	42
GOODNIGHT, NEBRASKA	page	44

INDEX BY GENRE

Fiction (continued)

THE HOURS	page	46
HUMMINGBIRD HOUSE	page	48
I CAPTURE THE CASTLE	page	50
LEARNING FROM HANNAH	page	56
LIVING ON THE EDGE	page	58
THE LOVE OF A GOOD WOMAN	page	60
THE MANY LIVES AND SECRET SORROWS OF JOSEPHINE B.	page	62
MR. PHILLIPS	page	64
PEARS ON A WILLOW TREE	page	66
PEEL MY LOVE LIKE AN ONION	page	68
A PLACE WITHOUT TWILIGHT	page	70
PRETZEL LOGIC	page	72
THE RED TENT	page	74
THE SKY UNWASHED	page	80
STYGO	page	84
SUGAR LAND	page	86
SUMMER AT THE RESORT	page	88
SUNDAY YOU LEARN HOW TO BOX	page	90
TALES OF PASSION, TALES OF WOE	page	92
UNFORGOTTEN	page	94
WHERE RIVER TURNS TO SKY	page	96
ZABELLE	page	98

About *Reading Group Choices*

This publication, the sixth edition of *Reading Group Choices*, was developed and produced by Paz & Associates, whose mission is to join with publishers and booksellers to develop resources and skills that promote books and reading.

Books for potential inclusion are recommended by book group members, librarians, booksellers, and publishers. All submissions are then reviewed by an Advisory Group of book industry professionals, to ensure the "discussibility" of each title. Once a title is approved for inclusion, publishers are then asked to underwrite production costs, so that copies of *Reading Group Choices* can be distributed for the cost of shipping and handling alone.

Twenty thousand copies of *Reading Group Choices* are distributed annually to bookstores, libraries, and directly to book groups. Back issues are available only in photocopy form, at $5.95 each. Titles from previous issues are also posted on our website at *readinggroupchoices.com*.

For additional copies of this publication, please call your local library or independent bookstore, or you may contact us at the address and phone number below. We will be happy to ship copies to you directly, or let you know of a bookstore in your area that has obtained copies of *Reading Group Choices*. Please be advised, however, that some bookstores will offer copies free of charge as a customer service, while others may charge the single-copy price of $5.95 each. Quantities are limited.

For more information, please visit our website at:
www.readinggroupchoices.com

Or contact:

Paz & Associates
2106 Twentieth Avenue South
Nashville, TN 37212-4312

800/260-8605 — phone
615/298-2303 — phone
615/298-9864 — fax
dpaz@pazbookbiz.com — email

About Paz & Associates

The mission of Paz & Associates is to serve the bookselling community by empowering people and organizations with new skills and insights that significantly increase their ability to serve customers. We offer a variety of products and services to bookstores, publishers, and other book-related organizations, including the following:

- consulting with prospective and current retail booksellers on marketing, human resources, store design, merchandising, and business operations, including financial analysis and inventory selection and control

- the quarterly newsletters *Independent Bookselling Today!* and *The FrontLine Bookseller*

- *The Reader's Edge* bookstore newsletter marketing program

- *Opening a Bookstore: The Essential Planning Guide*

- *The Retail Training Center for Booksellers*, located within The Renaissance Center in Dickson, Tennessee

- *The Training Guide to FrontLine Bookselling*

- *Exceptional FrontLine Bookselling: It's All About Service*, a 60 minute training video

- *Greeting Cards* with designs to celebrate books and reading

For more information, please visit our website at:
www.pazbookbiz.com

Or contact:

Paz & Associates
2106 Twentieth Avenue South
Nashville, TN 37212-4312

800/260-8605 – phone
615/298-2303 – phone
615/298-9864 – fax
dpaz@pazbookbiz.com – email

Visit us online...

The #1 Internet Resource for Book Groups

www.readinggroupchoices.com

Looking for other great book selections for your book group? Want to know if guides are available for titles you have in mind? Want the latest scoop on newly released discussible books?

LOOK WHAT'S NEW — See what publishers have in store; get the inside scoop on new discussible books.

DIRECTORY OF AVAILABLE GUIDES — Search a comprehensive list of over 550 titles with discussion guides—print more than 200 directly from the site.

TIPS ON STARTING A BOOK GROUP — Thinking about starting a book group? Here are some quick tips and ideas to get you going.

GUIDANCE FOR GROUP LEADERS — Expert advice on running a successful book discussion group.

PAST EDITIONS — Past editions of *Reading Group Choices* you can browse and download.

For resources ready for you to use on the world-wide web, visit www.readinggroupchoices.com